Cooking for Heart and Soul

Cooking for Heart and Soul

100 Delicious Low-Fat Recipes from San Francisco's Top Chefs
A Cookbook to Benefit the San Francisco Food Bank

Compiled and Edited by
Stanley Eichelbaum

Photography by
Joyce Oudkerk Pool

Foreword by
Paul Ash

Preface by
Jean Weininger

CHRONICLE BOOKS

SAN FRANCISCO

Library of Congress Cataloging-in-Publication Data
Cooking for heart and soul: 101 delicious low-fat recipes
    from San Francisco's top chefs: a cookbook to benefit the
    San Francisco Food Bank / edited and compiled by Stanley
    Eichelbaum; photography by Joyce Oudkerk Pool.
        p.   cm.
    Includes index.
    ISBN 0-8118-0824-6
    1. Cookery. 2. Low-fat diet–Recipes. 3. Low-calorie
diet–Recipes. I. Eichelbaum, Stanley.
    TX714.C6544 1995
    641.5´638–dc20   95-1572
                                                              CIP

Photography: Joyce Oudkerk Pool
Food Stylist: Pouké
Design: Palomine

Printed in Hong Kong.

ISBN 0-8118-0824-6

Distributed in Canada by Raincoast Books,
8680 Cambie Street,
Vancouver, B.C. V6P 6M9

10 9 8 7 6 5 4 3 2 1

Chronicle Books
275 Fifth Street
San Francisco, CA 94103

The recipe on page 36 is from *The Supper Book* by Marion
Cunningham. Copyright © 1992 by Marion Cunningham.
Reprinted by permission of Alfred A. Knopf, Inc.

The recipe on page 41 is from *Adventures in the Kitchen* by
Wolfgang Puck. Copyright © 1991 by Wolfgang Puck. Reprinted
by permission of Random House.

The recipes on pages 41 and 111 are from *Everybody's Wokking* by
Martin Yan. Copyright © 1991 by Martin Yan. Reprinted by
permission of Harlow & Ratner.

The recipe on page 55 is from *China Moon Cookbook* by Barbara
Tropp. Copyright © 1992 by Barbara Tropp. Reprinted by
permission of Workman Publishing Co., Inc.

The recipe on page 52 is adapted from *New American Classics* by
Jeremiah Tower. Copyright © 1986 by Jeremiah Tower. Reprinted
by permission of HarperCollins Publishers.

The recipe on page 70 is from *Italy in Small Bites* by Carol Field.
Copyright © 1993 by Carol Field. Reprinted by permission of
William Morrow and Co., Inc.

The recipe on page 90 is from *Cold Spaghetti at Midnight* by
Maggie Waldron. Copyright © 1993 by Maggie Waldron. Reprinted
by permission of William Morrow and Co., Inc.

To David, an exceptional chef and dear friend

✳

Acknowledgments

I wish to thank the personnel of the different San Francisco markets that I frequented, especially the staffs of the Chinese, Japanese and Hispanic food stores, who gave me friendly advice and assistance in locating imported ingredients during the recipe-testing period of this project. I'm also grateful to Terry and Peter Flannery of Bryan's meat, poultry and seafood market for their generous help and information about unusual seafood. My thanks, too, to Andy Powning of Greenleaf Produce for his patient and knowledgeable answers to questions about obscure produce. My special thanks to Kathleen Meeker, Mary Lonergan, Carol Francoz, Martha Nell Beatty, Gretta Wark, and J.T. Mann for their enthusiastic help with recipe testing. Finally, I would like to express my gratitude to the San Francisco Food Bank for giving me the opportunity to work on this cookbook as a fund-raiser to benefit their very worthy programs. Joyce Oudkerk Pool and Pouké would like to thank the following people for their help, love and support: Brenda, Charles, Chloe, Erez and Gibson.

Contents

Foreword

When the San Francisco Food Bank was founded in 1980, hunger and poverty were less visible than they are today, and so were we. Operating from the back of a truck, volunteers picked up unsold but still edible food that wholesalers, retailers and packers would normally throw away. They distributed the food to a few service agencies that existed to provide meals to people in crisis.

The number of hungry and homeless in San Francisco has multiplied every year and the Food Bank has kept pace with the growing need by increasing its capacity and services. Currently, more than ninety thousand adults and children in San Francisco—approximately one person out of every eight—live below the poverty line and are at risk of hunger. We at the Food Bank regard this fact as more than an abstract statistic. It represents a real battle against a real enemy with real victims. The people behind the statistics make our work essential.

The numbers comprise more than the unemployed and dispossessed. A family whose income does not cover basic living expenses turns to the Food Bank to receive supplemental food supplies. A low-income senior receives biweekly groceries from the Food Bank to help make ends meet. A person struggling to overcome drug or alcohol addiction receives our food supplies as part of a comprehensive recovery program. The recipients include battered women and their children, and persons living with AIDS. There are homeless people, too, who stand in line at a soup kitchen for a meal made with our provisions.

The Food Bank is San Francisco's largest distributor of food to the needy. As a central clearinghouse for donated food, it works with supermarkets, farmers and other suppliers to recover food that would otherwise go to waste.

Staff members and volunteers sort, clean and rewrap produce, packaged goods and dairy products to provide a consistent supply of nutritious food to San Francisco's hungry. Each year, we distribute approximately four million pounds of food through a network of more than three hundred direct-service agencies. Through this collaboration, the Food Bank saves the agencies thousands of dollars in food costs, allowing them to channel these funds into other services for the poor.

Our efforts would not be possible without community support, whether through food drives or fund-raising events. We're especially grateful to San Francisco's celebrated chefs for donating their talent and time to benefit our cause, and to all those who purchase this extraordinary cookbook, the proceeds from which will be used to carry on our hunger-relief work.

PAUL ASH
EXECUTIVE DIRECTOR
SAN FRANCISCO FOOD BANK

Preface

Fat: We can't live with it and we can't live without it.
Or so it seems.

By now, we're well aware of the perils of too much dietary fat, and many of us are trying hard to cut our fat intake. Fat has been linked not only to heart disease, the number-one killer in America, but also to various cancers and obesity—itself associated with an increased risk for heart disease, diabetes and early death.

Of course, fat isn't all bad. We need to eat some polyunsaturated fat (a little will do) to stay alive. We need it for normal growth and development, for hormone production and for healthy skin and hair. Fat also facilitates absorption of the fat-soluble vitamins (A, D, E and K). And fat contributes to the good taste of food and makes us feel that we really ate something ("satiety value").

Cholesterol, too, has many essential functions, even though the waxy, fat-like substance has an unsavory reputation because of its presence in artery-clogging plaque. Our bodies make more than enough cholesterol to meet our needs, but, as we know all too well, it's also in our food.

A Quick Review of Fats in Food

Fats in food are combinations of different fatty acids. Most saturated fatty acids raise blood cholesterol, particularly the LDL ("bad") cholesterol linked to increased risk of heart disease. Saturated fats, solid at room temperature, are found in meat, poultry and dairy products, as well as in tropical oils such as palm and coconut. Dietary cholesterol—found only in animal products, such as meat, poultry, eggs, fish and dairy products—can also increase blood cholesterol, but not nearly so much as saturated fat does.

Unsaturated fatty acids, on the other hand, lower blood cholesterol. Both polyunsaturated and monounsaturated fats (oils) are liquid at room temperature. Polyunsaturated fat—the predominant fat in vegetable oils such as corn, safflower and soybean—has fallen out of favor in recent years because it lowers HDL ("good") as well as LDL ("bad") cholesterol. Also, studies on animals have raised concerns that large amounts of polyunsaturates might lead to cell damage from the highly reactive chemical substances know as free radicals and even from cancer.

The "omega-3s," which are polyunsaturates in fish oils, have made a big splash of late because of several possible benefits, including decreased chance of blood clots. However, it's better to get omega-3s by eating fish two or three times a week than by taking supplements, whose safety has not been established.

Unquestionably, monounsaturated fat is today's fat of choice. Plentiful in olive and canola oil (as well as avocados, sesame seeds, almonds and other seeds and nuts), the monos lower LDL but not HDL cholesterol, and don't have the potential drawbacks of the polys.

It should also be pointed out that monounsaturated fat is a key player in the so-called Mediterranean diet, an eating pattern low in animal fat and high in olive oil, which is thought to contribute to the low heart-disease rates in Greece and southern Italy. This trendy diet has added appeal—and controversy—because it includes an optional glass or so of wine, which may have beneficial effects on blood cholesterol.

The last stop on this whirlwind tour of fats is trans fatty acids, formed when unsaturated fatty acids in vegetable oils are hardened by hydrogenation. These fats wend their way into many processed foods, including crackers, cookies, pastries, cakes, doughnuts, French fries, potato chips, puddings, peanut butter, vegetable shortening and margarine. Trans fats behave like saturates, and may turn out to be just as detrimental, but the last word is not yet in on these high-profile fats.

PRACTICALLY SPEAKING

On the average, 34 percent of our calories come from fat, 12 percent from saturated fat. So we still have a way to go to reach the widely accepted goal of 30 percent, with only 10 percent from saturates, or even lower, as some health professionals recommend.

Eating fat-reduced products that mimic the taste and "mouth feel" of fat is one approach. But in the long run, it's better to reeducate your taste buds to appreciate foods naturally low in fat. By cutting back on high-fat food for a while, before long you may actually come to prefer less fatty food.

And that's where this book comes in: Top chefs of the San Francisco Bay area have generously contributed recipes which are delicious, as well as generally low in fat, and Stanley Eichelbaum has put them all together in a very palatable package.

Not every recipe has less than 30 percent of its calories from fat, but that doesn't mean it can't be part of a healthful, low-fat diet. The 30 percent figure is a general guideline that should average out over a day, or several days, and need not apply to any one dish or meal.

Fat is calorically dense, with 9 calories per gram, compared to 4 calories per gram of carbohydrate or protein. To figure out the percent of calories from fat in a serving (or a meal, or a day's diet), first calculate the number of fat calories by multiplying the grams of fat by 9. Then, divide the number of fat calories by the number of total calories and multiply by 100 to get the percent. Again, it's not the percent of calories from fat in any one dish that's important, but the percent in the overall daily diet.

The new food label that appears on processed food is an important tool to help you get a handle on the fat in your diet. The label has ushered in a reference point called the "daily value," which suggests an upper limit of 65 grams of fat, 20 grams of saturated fat and 300 milligrams of cholesterol in a 2,000-calorie diet (for a 2,500-calorie diet, it's 80 grams fat, 25 grams saturated fat and the same 300 milligrams cholesterol). Many fresh foods, such as fruits, vegetables, raw fish, meat and poultry, have no labels, but are covered by a voluntary program in which nutrition information is provided on brochures or signs posted nearby.

The food label doesn't as yet list grams of the suspect trans fat, but you can get clues as to its presence by checking ingredient lists for "partially hydrogenated oils." As for butter and margarine, both are virtually all fat, so use as little as possible. There's considerably less fat and fewer trans fats—sometimes none—in the new "light" spreads and blends, which may appeal to some. And while we're encouraged to use heart-friendly oils, such as olive and canola, don't get carried away. They're still fat.

The bottom line for healthful eating remains: Eat less fat. Go easy on the red meat and full-fat dairy products. Eat fish and skinless white-meat poultry, if you like. And make grains, vegetables and fruits the centerpiece of your diet.

This cookbook proves that nutritious eating doesn't have to be boring. The gourmet recipes will tantalize your taste buds as well as contribute to two worthy causes: the San Francisco Food Bank and your good health.

JEAN WEININGER
PH.D. IN NUTRITION, UC BERKELEY
HEALTH COLUMNIST, SAN FRANCISCO CHRONICLE

No doubt about it, fat has become the archvillain of the nineties. Warnings about the hazards of dietary fat have been relentless, and our preoccupation with low-fat, nonfat and reduced-fat food has infiltrated our language, revolutionized our diets and changed our cooking habits. I can think of nothing that has penetrated the culinary world with such resounding impact since the Cuisinart charged into our kitchens in the seventies.

The subject is so pervasive that no other theme came to mind when I sat down to plan this work on behalf of the San Francisco Food Bank. This cookbook will therefore explore some unique, exciting and novel ways of lowering the fat in cooking. But unlike so many other recent works on lean, healthy cuisine, ours does not deal with the kind of diet food that tends to be flat and flavorless. Nor does it encroach on the rigid terrain of heart-healthy cookbooks assembled by well-meaning physicians whose vegetarian, virtually fat-free diets are generally dull and difficult to maintain, prompting culinary maven Alice Waters to remark, caustically but aptly, "Looking at food as preventative medicine is a disappointingly narrow perspective."

Our book focuses on the subject of healthy food from the standpoint of the gifted and resourceful chefs of northern California. We asked these chefs, who include some of the most celebrated in the country, how they were cutting back on fat without sacrificing flavor. How do they remove cream, butter, salt and other flavor-packed indulgences from their cooking and still come up with great-tasting food?

The chefs responded with gratifying fervor and submitted a remarkable assortment of imaginative and original recipes for delicious food which will add considerable panache to your culinary repertoire. While the fat content of the recipes is variable and occasionally exceeds the 30 percent guideline of calories from fat (based on a daily total of 2,000 calories) recommended by the U.S. Department of Agriculture and by the American Heart Association, most fall well below that level. It's therefore possible to splurge on a higher-fat dish and balance it with low-fat dishes to keep within the overall daily fat limit.

Not surprisingly, most of the chefs sent recipes for vegetable, fish and poultry dishes, which contain a minimum of fat and artery-clogging cholesterol. We've included a few meat dishes, but these call for very lean meat (e.g., venison, veal and pork tenderloin), prepared with almost no added fat.

However, it should be pointed out that the 30 percent fat guideline can be tricky and even misleading, since a good many patently healthful vegetable dishes are so low in calories that the addition of just a small amount of oil gives them a surprisingly high percentage of fat. For example, a ratatouille consisting of nothing but vegetables is cooked with 2 tablespoons of olive oil, and though it has only 95 calories per serving, it chalks up 42 percent calories from fat, since the vegetables have so few calories. Similarly, a summer vegetable salad with 1 tablespoon of olive oil has 57 calories but registers 53 percent calories from fat. Yet both dishes are indisputably healthy and need not be shunned, since they contain a negligible amount of saturated fat and no cholesterol. Each recipe in the cookbook has been nutritionally analyzed for calories, protein, carbohydrates, fat, cholesterol and sodium. The amounts are approximate and the sodium content includes only measured amounts of salt rather than salt to taste.

The purpose of this work is to show how to cook with a minimum of fat and still produce appealing food that explodes with flavor. The chefs have done this in bold and fascinating ways, most often by reinventing sauces, or replacing them with relishes, salsas and chutneys. The sauces are light, vibrant and generally fat free. There are salmon recipes, for example, that demonstrate methods of preparing this innately oily fish (38 percent of calories from fat) with no added fat so it can be enjoyed without remorse. You'll find assertive flavors bursting from sauces made of fresh fruit and exotic herbs and spices that exemplify the multiethnic nature of San Francisco's cuisine. The Asian influence is particularly strong, and if certain recipes contain ingredients you've never heard of (e.g., Sichuan peppercorns and kaffir lime leaves), you'll probably enjoy exploring the Asian markets to seek them out. But in many instances, you may not have to go farther than your local supermarket, since most have ethnic sections stocked with all kinds of unfamiliar items.

STANLEY EICHELBAUM

about the chefs

Joey Altman

Joey Altman was fourteen when he started cooking in Catskill Mountain resort hotels. Traveling to France, he apprenticed in restaurants in Brittany and Lyons. Since coming to California, he has been the chef of San Francisco's Caribbean-style Miss Pearl's Jam House and the more eclectic Palace restaurant in suburban Sunnyvale.

ROASTED TOMATO CHUTNEY (PAGE 130)

Flo Braker

Flo Braker resides in Palo Alto, California, and has taught baking techniques and pastry-making across the country for the past twenty years. Her column on baking appears regularly in the *San Francisco Chronicle.* She is the author of *The Simple Art of Perfect Baking* (Chapters, 1985) and *Sweet Miniatures* (Morrow, 1991).

FRUIT SPONGE CAKE AND SUMMER PUDDING

(PAGE 133)

Gloria Ciccarone-Nehls

Gloria Ciccarone-Nehls considers that she grew up in a kitchen, having helped with cooking chores during her early teens in her father's restaurant in Bethel, Connecticut. On graduating from the Culinary Institute of America, in Hyde Park, New York, she was engaged as sous-chef of the Big Four restaurant in San Francisco's Huntington Hotel. She has been the executive chef since 1981 and has made a specialty of big game cuisine, from alligator to ostrich.

BEET SOUP WITH GINGER AND CHIVE CREAM

(PAGE 36)

COLD POACHED HALIBUT WITH GOLDEN PEPPER

COULIS AND PAPAYA-MINT RELISH (PAGE 101)

Margie Conard and Dana Tommasino

Margie Conard and Dana Tommasino grew up in southern California and came to San Francisco to attend the California Culinary Academy. After graduating, Conard worked at Postrio and Tommasino at Greens. In 1993, they became co-chefs and partners in Woodward's Garden, a small but highly esteemed San Francisco restaurant.

ARTICHOKE STUFFED WITH PINE NUTS
AND CURRANTS WITH MEYER LEMON VINAIGRETTE
(PAGE 48)

David Coyle

David Coyle attended culinary school in his native Dublin prior to holding chef's positions in London in such top hotels as the Savoy, Dorchester and Grosvenor House. He then spent ten years as the private chef of the Duke and Duchess of Bedford at Woburn Abbey. Since 1980, he has been a San Francisco resident, working as the chef of the Mansion Hotel and operating his own catering firm, Culinary Art, Inc.

PINK GRAPEFRUIT MERINGUE WITH RASPBERRIES
AND HAZELNUTS (PAGE 139)

Bruce Cost

Bruce Cost, author of *Asian Ingredients* (Morrow, 1988) and *Ginger East to West* (Addison-Wesley, 1989), has devoted over twenty years to cooking, teaching and writing about Asian food. He operated a celebrated San Francisco restaurant, Monsoon, from 1989 to 1992, and then opened Ginger Island in Berkeley and Ginger Club in Palo Alto.

HAND-SHREDDED EGGPLANT
WITH SESAME SEEDS (PAGE 126)

Ercolino Crugnale

Despite his impressive Italian name, Ercolino Crugnale was born in El Paso and raised in Denver. He is a graduate of the Culinary Institute of America in Hyde Park, New York, and began his career as chef tournant at the Salishan Lodge in Gleneden, Oregon. He came to California in 1986 to be the chef of Los Olivos Grand Hotel near Santa Barbara. He then became the executive chef at the Monterey Plaza Hotel in Monterey and the executive sous-chef at the Hotel Bel Air in Los Angeles. Since 1992, he has been the executive chef of Fournou's Ovens in San Francisco's Stouffer Stanford Court Hotel.

MANDARIN QUAIL WITH GINGER JUICE AND
CINNAMON OIL (PAGE 60)

Marion Cunningham

Marion Cunningham writes about cooking for the *San Francisco Chronicle* and *Los Angeles Times*. She lives in Walnut Creek, across the Bay from San Francisco, and was responsible for the complete revision of *The Fannie Farmer Cookbook* (Knopf, 1979). She is the author of *The Fannie Farmer Baking Book*, *The Breakfast Book* and *The Supper Book* (Knopf, 1984, 1987 and 1992).

CHINESE SPICY SOUP (PAGE 36)

Gary Danko

Raised in Massena, New York, Gary Danko received his chef's training at the Culinary Institute of America in Hyde Park, New York. In 1984, he became a disciple of Madeleine Kamman and spent two years studying with the French cooking teacher and author in California, New Hampshire and France. For the next five years, he was chef of the acclaimed restaurant in the Château Souverain Winery in Geyserville, California. In 1991, he helped open the San Francisco Ritz-Carlton and is presently chef of the hotel's top-ranking Dining Room.

ASPARAGUS WITH RED ONION VINAIGRETTE (PAGE 78)
CHOLESTEROL-FREE RASPBERRY SOUFFLÉ (PAGE 142)

Narsai M. David

Narsai M. David is a popular TV and radio personality who appears as resident chef on *Mornings at 2* on KTVU, Oakland, and comments on food and wine on KCBS Radio, San Francisco. He was a partner in Berkeley's Potluck restaurant from 1959 to 1970 and the owner of Narsai's restaurant in nearby Kensington from 1970 to 1984. He writes a food column for the *San Francisco Chronicle* and is the author of *Monday Night at Narsai's* (Simon and Schuster, 1987).

CHICKEN AND DUMPLINGS (PAGE 115)
WINTER VEGETABLE CASSEROLE (PAGE 121)

Peter DeMarais

Peter DeMarais is a native San Franciscan descended from a long line of chefs. His French great-grandfather, Pierre Epinot, came from Lyons in 1892 to be the chef of San Francisco's Palace Hotel. DeMarais works at the same historic hotel, now the Sheraton-Palace. He started as executive sous-chef in 1990 and moved up to the post of executive chef in 1993. Prior to that, he was the chef at the Cafe Majestic. He twice won first prize for recipes entered in a health-food contest organized by the Oakland Cancer Education and Prevention Center. He is also a competitive marathon runner.

SEAFOOD MOSAIC WITH CRANBERRY SYRUP, WATERCRESS COULIS AND BEET AND FENNEL SALAD (PAGE 53)
QUINCE AND PEAR WHOLE WHEAT CRÊPES WITH BLUEBERRY SAUCE (PAGE 136)

Jeanne-Pierre Dubray

Having trained as a chef in his hometown of Château Renault in the Loire Valley and in Paris, Jean-Pierre Dubray came to California in 1980 to work at La Vie en Rose restaurant in the Orange County town of Brea. In 1984, he became the executive chef of the Ritz-Carlton Hotel in Laguna Niguel and subsequently at the Ritz-Carlton in Rancho Mirage. Since 1991, he has been the executive chef of the Ritz-Carlton in San Francisco.

VEAL NOISETTES WITH CITRUS JUICE
AND APPLE MOUSSE (PAGE 119)

Stanley Eichelbaum

Stanley Eichelbaum is a journalist and chef who spent eighteen years as a film and theater critic of the *San Francisco Examiner* before acquiring a professional chef's degree from the California Culinary Academy. He operated two San Francisco restaurants, Eichelbaum & Co. and Cafe Majestic. He has been a cooking teacher at San Francisco City College and a food columnist for the *San Francisco Chronicle*. He is the editor of *The Open Hand Celebration Cookbook* (Pocket Books, 1991).

POULE-AU-POT UPDATED (PAGE 114)

Judith and Rebecca Ets-Hokin

Judith Ets-Hokin is the author of *The San Francisco Dinner Party Cookbook* (Houghton Mifflin, 1975) and *The Home Chef: Fine Cooking Made Simple* (Celestial Arts, 1988). She is the primary instructor of Judith Ets-Hokin's Homechef Cooking School, founded in San Francisco in 1973. Judith's daughter, Rebecca Ets-Hokin, studied at the Ritz-Escoffier and Cordon Bleu cooking schools in Paris, and is the director of her mother's flourishing school.

BORN-AGAIN MASHED POTATOES WITH
YOGURT CHEESE (PAGE 127)
CHOCOLATE ESPRESSO DECADENCE (PAGE 133)

Carol Field

Although Carol Field lives in San Francisco with her architect husband, she has spent a good part of her life exploring Italy and its food. She has written four books on the subject, *The Hill Towns of Italy* (Dutton, 1983), *The Italian Baker* (Harper & Row, 1985), *Celebrating Italy* (Morrow, 1990) and *Italy in Small Bites* (Morrow, 1993). She is also the author of *Focaccia* (Chronicle, 1995).

COOL SUMMER VEGETABLE SALAD (PAGE 70)

Barbara Figueroa

A native New Yorker, Barbara Figueroa took classes with James Beard at his cooking school in Manhattan prior to an apprenticeship in France under chef André Daguin in Auch, Gascony. Back in New York, she worked with Alain Sailhac at Le Cirque and Jonathan Waxman at Jams, and then headed for Los Angeles to work with Wolfgang Puck at Spago. In Seattle, she was executive chef of the Hunt Club in the Sorrento Hotel. In San Francisco, she was chef de cuisine of Victor's, the noted dining room on the thirty-second floor of the St. Francis Hotel. She is presently doing consulting work.

CHILLED GOLDEN BELL PEPPER SOUP (PAGE 37)
GRILLED STURGEON WITH CHILI-SOY GLAZE, BABY
BOK CHOY AND NORI CRISPS (PAGE 100)

Margaret Fox

Native Californian Margaret Fox has overseen the much esteemed Cafe Beaujolais in the north coast town of Mendocino since 1977. Her restaurant is noted for its creative breakfasts and baked goods, and, in recent years, for dinners by her chef-husband Christopher Kump. Her cookbooks, *Cafe Beaujolais* and *Morning Food* (Ten Speed , 1984 and 1990), were written with John Bear.

TOFU-VEGETABLE SCRAMBLE (PAGE 65)

Thom Fox

Thom Fox was raised in Pittsburgh, Pennsylvania, and worked in the steel mills before getting into the kitchen. He received his chef's training at Johnson & Wales University in Providence, Rhode Island. Since moving to San Francisco in 1985, he has cooked at the Fog City Diner, China Moon and Eddie Jacks, and, as executive chef, has overseen the Mexican and Southwest cuisine at the Corona Bar & Grill, which was renamed Abiquiu in 1994.

GRILLED SALMON WITH ANCHO-SESAME VINAIGRETTE,
ROASTED BUTTERNUT SQUASH AND
BLUE-CORN TORTILLA CRISPS (PAGE 106)

Eric Gallanter

Eric Gallanter was the executive chef and operations manager of the Marlboro Inn in Montclair, New Jersey, before he moved to San Francisco in 1993 to open Eric in the downtown Rincon Center. He is a graduate of the Culinary Institute of America in Hyde Park, New York. His wife Joanna Rees-Gallanter is co-proprietor and business manager of his restaurant.

POACHED SEA BASS WITH TOMATO WATER
AND SPRING VEGETABLES (PAGE 99)

Elka Gilmore

After cooking in an Italian restaurant in Boston and serving a six-month apprenticeship in the south of France, Texas-born Elka Gilmore rose to prominence in Los Angeles at Camelions with a menu of Franco-Italian cuisine. From there, she moved to Tumbleweed in Beverly Hills, winning acclaim for her Southwest food. In 1991, she settled in San Francisco and launched a unique Japanese-influenced seafood restaurant eponymously named Elka in the Miyako Hotel. She has since assumed a second post as executive chef at Liberté, where the food has a French slant.

TUNA TARTARE ON NORI ROUNDS (PAGE 49)
CORIANDER-ENCRUSTED AHI TUNA WITH VEGETABLES
AND GLASS NOODLES (PAGE 97)

Anne and David Gingrass

Anne and David Gingrass met while studying at the Culinary Institute of America in Hyde Park, New York. Their restaurant alliance started in 1986 at Wolfgang Puck's Spago in Los Angeles. In 1989, they helped Puck open his San Francisco bastion, Postrio, and were the executive chefs for six years, until they opened their own San Francisco restaurant, Hawthorne Lane, in 1995.

STIR-FRIED GARLIC CHICKEN WITH CILANTRO (PAGE 66)

Joyce Goldstein

Joyce Goldstein cooked at Chez Panisse in Berkeley and ran a San Francisco cooking school prior to opening her celebrated San Francisco restaurant, Square One, in 1984. She is the author of *The Mediterranean Kitchen* (Morrow, 1989) and *Back to Square One* (Morrow, 1992). She writes a column for the *San Francisco Chronicle* and travels nationwide as a teacher and lecturer.

CURRIED BROCCOLI SOUP (PAGE 39)
GRILLED FISH IN TURKISH MARINADE OF YOGURT,
CORIANDER, CARDAMOM AND LEMON (PAGE 113)

Joel Guillon

Joel Guillon received his formal chef's training in France, working with such notable chefs as Alain Chapel, Marc Meneau and Antoine Westermann. He joined the French-owned Meridien hotel chain and came to San Francisco in 1983 to be the executive chef of the newly built Meridien. He retained his post when the Meridien was purchased by All Nippon Airways in 1992 and renamed the ANA Hotel.

SWORDFISH WITH PINEAPPLE CHUTNEY AND
BROILED BANANA (PAGE 105)

Rick Hackett

Rick Hackett is a graduate of the Culinary Institute of America in Hyde Park, New York. After cooking for two years at Le Pavillon in Washington, D.C., he came to California in 1979 and worked at Berkeley's Chez Panisse and Oakland's Bay Wolf and Olivetto. In 1992, he acquired San Francisco's renowned Enrico's restaurant with his wife Meredith Melville and Mark McLeod as partners.

SALMON AL FORNO WITH WHITE BEANS (PAGE 109)

Jay Harlow

Jay Harlow worked as a chef at San Francisco's Hayes Street Grill and Berkeley's Santa Fe Bar & Grill before embarking on a career as a food writer. He writes a column on seafood for the *San Francisco Chronicle* and, in 1990, he and his wife Elaine Ratner started the publishing house of Harlow & Ratner. His own cookbooks include *The California Seafood Cookbook* (Aris, 1983), *The Grilling Book* (Aris, 1987), *Shrimp* (Chronicle, 1989), *The Art of the Sandwich* (Chronicle, 1990) and *Beer Cuisine* (Harlow & Ratner, 1991).

STEAMED WHOLE ROCKFISH WITH BASIL
AND TOMATO (PAGE 110)

Reed Hearon

Reed Hearon grew up in Austin, Texas, where an early love of Mexican food grew into a scholarly and pragmatic passion. After extensive travels in Mexico to study the cuisine, he worked as a chef at Denver's Rattlesnake Club and Santa Fe's Coyote Cafe, and then won wide recognition as executive chef of San Francisco's upscale Mexican-style Corona Bar & Grill. In 1993, he scored a phenomenal success with two San Francisco restaurants of his own. He opened the Mediterranean-inspired Restaurant Lulu and the contemporary Mexican Café Marimba. He is the author of *Salsa* (Chronicle, 1993).

SOPA RANCHERA (PAGE 43)

Robert Helstrom

Robert Helstrom moved to southern California from Fort Wayne, Indiana, in 1980, and cooked at such restaurants as Hemingway in Newport Beach and Pave in Corona del Mar. In 1988, he came to San Francisco, where he is presently the executive chef of Kuleto's, a popular Italian-style downtown restaurant.

POLENTA SOUFFLÉ WITH
GRILLED PORCINI MUSHROOMS (PAGE 91)

Gérald Hirigoyen

A native Basque, Gérald Hirigoyen grew up in Biarritz, France, and started cooking at age thirteen in a small pastry shop. He was eighteen when he went to Paris to apprentice with the renowned pastry chef and caterer, Jean Millet. A San Francisco resident since 1980, he has cooked in French restaurants such as Le Castel, Lafayette and Le St. Tropez. In 1991, he became the chef and co-owner of Fringale, which translates as "the urge to eat."

SPRING VEGETABLE SALAD (PAGE 70)
STEAMED HALIBUT WITH CARROTS AND CUMIN SAUCE
(PAGE 103)
CHARDONNAY SORBET (PAGE 145)

Ken Hom

Ken Hom was born in Tucson, Arizona, and has long made his home in Berkeley, but he travels the world as an eminent authority on Chinese cooking. He has conducted classes in Hong Kong, has been a restaurant consultant in San Francisco (he revamped the menu at Silks), Bangkok, Sydney, London and sundry other cities. His BBC-TV series, *Ken Hom's Chinese Cookery*, has been an international hit. His seven cookbooks range from *Chinese Technique* (Simon and Schuster, 1981) to *Ken Hom's Quick & Easy Chinese Cooking* (Chronicle, 1992).

AN EAST-MEETS-WEST SANDWICH (PAGE 57)

Barbara Karoff

Barbara Karoff is a free-lance food and travel writer who lives in San Francisco. She is the author of *South American Cooking: Foods and Feasts from the New World* (Addison-Wesley, 1989) and *The Little Southwest Cookbook* (Chronicle, 1993). She has conducted cooking demonstrations on cargo-passenger ships sailing around South America.

GUILT-FREE COOKIES (PAGE 139)

Donna Katzl

Donna Katzl was a Las Vegas dancer and acted small parts in films and TV sitcoms prior to embarking on a chef's career. She opened the Simply Scrumptious Cafe with her husband Frank Katzl in 1972 in San Francisco's Stonestown shopping mall. She then took time out for cooking classes with James Beard prior to opening the very successful Cafe for All Seasons in 1983 in San Francisco's West Portal district. Since 1990, the Katzles have operated a second Cafe for All Seasons in suburban San Mateo.

BUTTER LETTUCE AND SPINACH SALAD WITH
PINE NUTS AND ROASTED GARLIC-HONEY DRESSING
(PAGE 73)
PENNE RIGATE PASTA WITH BABY ARTICHOKES
AND SPINACH (PAGE 83)
VEGETARIAN NAPA CABBAGE ROLLS WITH
MOREL MUSHROOMS AND TOMATO-THYME SAUCE
(PAGE 123)

Paul Kavouksorian

Paul Kavouksorian is a native of Utica, New York, and a graduate of the Culinary Institute of America in Hyde Park. He cooked in several New York restaurants before coming to San Francisco in 1979 to work at the Clift Hotel. In 1983, he opened his own establishment, Picnix, a bistro and take-out food shop.

GREEN BEAN SALAD WITH FIRE WALNUTS (PAGE 76)

Hubert Keller

Hubert Keller was born in Alsace and trained under such notable French chefs as Paul Bocuse, Gaston Lenôtre and Roger Vergé. He is currently executive chef and managing partner of San Francisco's Fleur de Lys restaurant. Though known for his elaborate presentations, he makes a specialty of low-fat and vegetarian dishes. In July, 1993, he was invited to the White House as a consultant on low-fat food, and prepared three menus for President and Mrs. Clinton.

BONELESS CHICKEN BREAST ROLLED OVER
WILD MUSHROOMS AND SPINACH (PAGE 113)

David Kinch

David Kinch spent four years as sous-chef under Barry Wine at The Quilted Giraffe in New York. He came to San Francisco in 1988 to be the chef at Silks in the Mandarin Oriental Hotel. He went to Europe in 1990 for travel and work, and served under Marc Meneu at his three-star restaurant, L'Espérance, in northern Burgundy. In 1992, he became the executive chef at San Francisco's landmark restaurant, Ernie's.

GRILLED TUNA WITH VEGETABLE MIGNONETTE
(PAGE 97)
CRANBERRY SOUP WITH FRESH FRUIT (PAGE 142)

Gino Laghi

Gino Laghi was born in Lugo, the geographic center of the Emilia-Romagna region of northern Italy. He was introduced to the traditional dishes of the region in the kitchen of his mother's restaurant and brought them with him when he came to San Francisco in 1972 to cook at Modesto Lanzone's in Ghirardelli Square. Since 1990, he's been preparing the specialties of Emilia-Romagna as well as his own recipes in his restaurant, Laghi.

PASTA TUTTO FUNGHI (PAGE 81)

Paula LeDuc

Paula LeDuc is one of the San Francisco Bay area's top caterers. She came to cooking as a second career after working with the visually handicapped. She taught blind adolescents how to cook, and in her free time studied French cuisine with the noted East Bay cooking teacher, Ken Wolfe. She started her firm, Paula LeDuc Fine Catering, in 1980 and has done weddings, parties and special events for as many as 2,500 people. More recently, she opened a food-to-go division called Allez.

GRILLED PRAWNS WITH PAPAYA SALSA (PAGE 58)

Christopher L. Majer

Christopher L. Majer began his culinary career in New York in such restaurants as the Gotham Bar & Grill, Arcadia and The Quilted Giraffe. He came to San Francisco in 1987 to be the executive sous-chef at Campton Place. He is presently the executive chef at Splendido's, doing his interpretation of Mediterranean cuisine.

VEGETABLE CURRY WITH APPLE COUSCOUS

(PAGE 92)

Carlo Middione

Carlo Middione was born in Buffalo, New York, into a Sicilian family of restaurateurs and innkeepers. He is is a chef, author, teacher, television personality and owner of Vivande, a high-style Italian deli and café. His cookbooks include *Pasta! Cooking It, Loving It* (Chalmers, 1982) and *The Food of Southern Italy* (Morrow, 1987).

ROAST LOIN OF PORK WITH ORANGE, RED ONION, OREGANO AND MARSALA (PAGE 117)
RICOTTA AL CAFFÈ (PAGE 145)

Kelly Mills

Kelly Mills worked fourteen years as a chef for the Four Seasons hotel chain, initially at the Four Seasons in Vancouver, then at the Ritz-Carlton in Chicago and, for seven years, as the executive chef of the Clift Hotel in San Francisco. In 1992, he opened his own restaurant and catering firm, Kelly's on Trinity, in San Francisco's Financial District.

TURKEY CHILI WITH TOMATILLOS (PAGE 63)

Mary Etta Moose

Mary Etta Moose was co-owner and executive chef of San Francisco's bustling Washington Square Bar & Grill from 1973 to 1989, and, with her husband Ed, opened the even more popular Moose's restaurant across the square in 1992. A specialist in low-fat cuisine, she has contributed recipes and articles to numerous cookbooks and magazines. She is the co-author with Brian St. Pierre of *The Flavor of North Beach* (Chronicle, 1981).

SARDINES WITH FENNEL, SWEET ONION, RAISINS AND SUN-DRIED TOMATO (PAGE 58)

RAGOÛT OF SPICED WHITE VEGETABLES WITH PRUNE WONTONS (PAGE 82)

Lenore Nolan-Ryan

Lenore Nolan-Ryan started cooking professionally as a teenager in Indianapolis by providing catered meals to the racing teams of the Indy 500. In 1976, she moved to San Francisco and polished her skills assisting the instructors at Tante Marie's Cooking School. In 1984, she and her husband Michael Ryan opened Ryan's restaurant and catering company.

PLUM, BASIL AND RED ONION SALAD (PAGE 73)

COMPOSED VEGETABLE SALAD WITH TONNATO SAUCE (PAGE 74)

PEACH, BLACKBERRY AND CASSIS COMPOTE (PAGE 129)

MARCY'S CHOCOLATE TRIFLE (PAGE 135)

Bradley Ogden

Bradley Ogden has gained a reputation for his inventive treatment of traditional American food. He was the chef of the American Restaurant in Kansas City, Missouri, until 1983, when he came to California to launch the restaurant in San Francisco's Campton Place Hotel. In 1989, he became the owner and executive chef of the Lark Creek Inn, in suburban Larkspur, and in 1993, he opened a second restaurant, One Market, in downtown San Francisco. He is the author of *Breakfast, Lunch and Dinner* (Random House, 1991).

SUMMER BEAN AND CORN SALAD (PAGE 76)

Kenneth Oringer

Kenneth Oringer is chef de cuisine of Silks, the noted restaurant in San Francisco's Mandarin Oriental Hotel. Raised in Paramus, New Jersey, he graduated from the Culinary Institute of America in Hyde Park, New York, and developed his distinctive style of French- and Asian-influenced food at Le Marquis de Lafayette in Boston, Terra in Greenwich, Connecticut, and the River Cafe in Brooklyn, New York.

CHILLED SPICED SALMON WITH SHAVED FENNEL AND BROCCOLI RABE (PAGE 107)

FRUIT NAPOLEON WITH FROZEN RASPBERRY YOGURT (PAGE 137)

Roland Passot

Roland Passot is a native of Lyons who left France in 1976 to work under chef Jean Blanchet at his renowned restaurant, Le Français, near Chicago. He moved to San Francisco in 1980 to be the chef at Le Castel and opened his own restaurant, La Folie, in 1988. He chose to call it La Folie, the French word for madness, because he felt that one has to be mad to go into the restaurant business. In 1994, he became a partner in a second operation in Marin County, the Left Bank, in Larkspur.

BOUILLABAISSE EN FOLIE (PAGE 96)
PEARS IN BEAUJOLAIS (PAGE 137)
GAZPACHO FRUIT SOUP (PAGE 143)

Cindy Pawlcyn

Cindy Pawlcyn has worked in restaurant kitchens since she was thirteen. She resides in Saint Helena, California, and is the executive chef and part owner of the remarkably successful Real Restaurant group, which operates six California restaurants—Mustards Grill and Tra Vigna in the Napa Valley. Buckeye Roadhouse in Mill Valley and Fog City Diner, Bistro Rôti and Bix in San Francisco—and the Buckhead Roadhouse in Chattanooga, Tennessee. She is the author of *The Fog City Diner Cookbook* (Ten Speed, 1993).

FLAT BREAD TOSTADA WITH BLACK BEANS, POACHED
EGG AND TOMATILLO SALSA (PAGE 63)

Wolfgang Puck

Wolfgang Puck is an Austrian-born chef who has built an immensely successful restaurant empire in California, first with Spago and Chinois on Main in Los Angeles, then with Postrio in San Francisco and Granita in Malibu. More recently, he opened another Spago restaurant in Las Vegas. He is the author of *The Wolfgang Puck Cookbook* and *Adventures in the Kitchen* (Random House, 1986 and 1991).

GAZPACHO WITH CRABMEAT (PAGE 41)

Julie Ann Ring

Julie Ann Ring is a Chicago native who made her reputation as a chef in San Francisco with the restaurant Rings. She then moved on to Julie's Supper Club as the supervising chef and part owner. She is presently the owner of the Cabaret-restaurant Heart and Soul.

RED MISO SOUP WITH SOBA NOODLES
AND SHIITAKE MUSHROOMS (PAGE 40)

Jacky Robert

Jacky Robert is a native of Normandy who trained as a chef at the renowned Parisian restaurants, Prunier and Maxim's. After coming to San Francisco in 1976, he was the executive chef at Ernie's and an instructor at the California Culinary Academy. He is presently the owner of two French restaurants: the elegant Amelio's and the adjacent, less formal Entrée des Artistes. In 1989, he was named Maître Cuisinier de France by the members of that exclusive chefs' society.

AMELIO'S VEGETABLE PÂTÉ (PAGE 47)

Judy Rodgers

Judy Rodgers is a native of St. Louis who developed her cooking skills as an exchange student in 1973 when she was placed with the Troisgros brothers at their renowned restaurant in Roanne, France. She worked as a chef at the Union Hotel in Benicia, California, and Chez Panisse in Berkeley. In 1987, she moved on to the Zuni Cafe in San Francisco as the chef and eventually, part owner.

ROASTED PIGEON WITH
WILD RICE-POLENTA TRIANGLES (PAGE 116)

Alain Rondelli

Alain Rondelli grew up in suburban Paris and was barely out of his teens when he served as a chef for French president Valéry Giscard d'Estaing at the Palais de l'Elysée. He moved on to become the first assistant to Marc Meneau at his three-star restaurant, L'Espérance, in Saint-Père-sous-Vézelay in northern Burgundy. He came to the United States on cooking tours with Meneau, and then settled in San Francisco, where he was the executive chef at Ernie's before opening his own restaurant, Alain Rondelli, in 1993.

RATATOUILLE RONDELLI (PAGE 126)

Michael Sabella

Michael Sabella is a graduate of the Culinary Institute of America in Hyde Park, New York. He presently serves as executive chef and partner of his family's hundred-year-old San Francisco seafood restaurant, A. Sabella, which boasts a sweeping view of Fisherman's Wharf from the Golden Gate to the Bay Bridge. Although his roots are Italian, he draws on a diverse array of cuisines when seeking out imaginative new ways to serve fresh seafood.

BROILED MAHIMAHI ON BLACK BEANS WITH
TOMATO-MANGO RELISH (PAGE 98)

Patrizio Sacchetto and Mark Herand

Patrizio Sacchetto and Mark Herand work as a team preparing Italian-inspired dishes at Umberto's restaurant in San Francisco, Sacchetto as executive chef and managing partner and Herand as chef de cuisine. Sacchetto received his training at the Maggia Culinary Academy in Stresa, Italy. Since coming to San Francisco in 1984, he has taught at the California Culinary Academy and served as chef at Harry's American Bar & Grill, the Blue Fox and Teatro. Herand is a Californian raised in Georgetown in the Sierra foothills. He studied under Sacchetto at the California Culinary Academy and was his sous-chef at Harry's American Bar & Grill prior to joining him at Umberto's in 1993.

WHOLE WHEAT PASTA WITH TOMATOES, OLIVES
AND BASIL (PAGE 81)
SWORDFISH WITH EGGPLANT CAPONATA (PAGE 105)
CHICKEN BREAST WITH PORCINI VINAIGRETTE
(PAGE 110)

Charles Saunders

Charles Saunders is a graduate of the Culinary Institute of America in Hyde Park, New York. He also trained in Switzerland, where he was the private chef of the U.S. ambassador in Bern. He came to the wine country of California in 1988 and worked for two-and-a-half years as executive chef at the Sonoma Mission Inn & Spa, developing recipes for healthy, organic spa food. Since 1992, he has been the chef-owner of the Eastside Oyster Bar & Grill in Sonoma.

BUTTERNUT AND ACORN SQUASH SOUP (PAGE 39)
LINGUINE WITH CHICKEN, SPINACH AND
MUSTARD-DILL SAUCE (PAGE 86)
CRANBERRY AND PINEAPPLE CHUTNEY (PAGE 129)

Julian Serrano

Julian Serrano is a native of Madrid, Spain. He trained as a chef in hotel restaurants on the Costa Del Sol and in the Canary Islands. He worked in restaurants in Switzerland, Germany and France before coming to San Francisco in 1984 as sous-chef at Masa's. He has been the executive chef since 1986, augmenting Masa's reputation as a world-class restaurant devoted to nouvelle French cuisine. In 1994, he received *San Francisco Focus* magazine's Chef of the Year award.

MEDALLIONS OF VENISON WITH
CARAMELIZED GREEN APPLES (PAGE 120)

Amey Shaw

Amey Shaw gained prominence as the executive chef of Bentley's Seafood Grill & Oyster Bar, a favored haunt of San Francisco's financial district. She first won recognition at the Fourth Street Grill in Berkeley and attracted more notice at the Maltese Grill in San Francisco prior to taking over at Bentley's in 1990. Named Outstanding Chef by Grand Master Chefs of America in March, 1989, she was guest chef for American Week in Cannes, France, later that year. She left Bentley's in 1994 to become a chef at Alta Plaza Restaurant.

GRILLED SCALLOPS WITH LENTILS, PIPERADE
AND BALSAMIC SYRUP (PAGE 50)

Lindsey Shere

Lindsey Shere joined Alice Waters in opening Chez Panisse, the ground-breaking Berkeley restaurant, in 1971, and has been the pastry chef ever since. She is the author of *Chez Panisse Desserts* (Random House, 1985) and is also co-owner with Kathleen Stewart of the Downtown Bakery and Creamery in Healdsburg, California.

MINTED CITRUS COMPOTE (PAGE 140)

Tom Switzer

Tom Switzer came to San Francisco from Indianapolis in 1981. He cooked Greek food at Asimakopoulos Cafe, sold and delivered fish for a wholesale firm called Gulfwater and cooked contemporary American food for chef-owner Julie Ring at Rings restaurant. He operated his own restaurant, Cafe Maisonette, for two years and, in 1992, rejoined Julie Ring as the executive chef of Julie's Supper Club.

DUNGENESS CRAB RAVIOLI WITH ASPARAGUS
AND ANISE BROTH (PAGE 85)

Jeremiah Tower

Jeremiah Tower came to California after studying architecture at Harvard University and changed his focus by entering the culinary field as chef and partner at Chez Panisse in Berkeley. Since then, he has been phenomenally successful as the owner of two San Francisco restaurants, Stars and Stars Cafe. In 1993, he branched out to the Napa Valley with Stars Oakville Cafe. He is the author of *New American Classics* (Harper & Row, 1986).

FISH PAILLARD WITH GINGER, GARLIC AND TOMATOES
(PAGE 52)

Irene Trias

Irene Trias is a native San Franciscan born into an Indian family from Bangalore. She was taught to cook by her grandmother and studied culinary techniques in India. She opened the Indian Oven with her husband Lia Kath in 1984 with a menu of California-Indian cuisine and, in 1992, a second San Francisco restaurant, Appam, specializing in claypot cookery of old India.

TANDOORI-STYLE BARBECUED PRAWNS
OVER MIXED GREENS (PAGE 59)

Barbara Tropp

Barbara Tropp is a scholar turned Chinese chef who was doing graduate work in Chinese poetry and art history when her interest shifted to cooking during a two-year stay in Chinese homes in Taiwan. In 1986, she opened China Moon Cafe in San Francisco. She is the author of *The Modern Art of Chinese Cooking* (Morrow, 1982) and *China Moon Cookbook* (Workman, 1992).

HOT AND SOUR SQUID (PAGE 55)

Patricia Unterman

Patricia Unterman is a chef-owner of the Hayes Street Grill, a popular San Francisco seafood house that opened in 1979. She was the *San Francisco Chronicle*'s restaurant critic for fifteen years and co-authored four editions of the guide, *Restaurants of San Francisco*, for Chronicle Books. Her latest work, *San Francisco for Food Lovers* (Chronicle, 1995), is a guide to the best restaurants, cafés and food stores in the Bay area.

CRAB AND MANGO SALAD (PAGE 78)

Lance Dean Velasquez

As founding chef of the immensely successful Moose's restaurant in San Francisco, Lance Dean Velasquez won accolades for his Italian-influenced contemporary American cuisine. A native of Sonoma, California, he has worked in the business for seventeen of his thirty years, first at his mother's café in Santa Rosa, then as sous-chef at Graziano's in Petaluma and the restaurant of the Château Souverain Winery in Geyserville. In San Francisco, he was sous-chef at the Ritz-Carlton Dining Room and Campton Place before working at Moose's from 1992 to 1994.

SHAVED FENNEL SALAD WITH BLOOD ORANGE
VINAIGRETTE AND CHEESE CROUTON (PAGE 72)
OXTAIL AND POTATO RAVIOLI IN VEGETABLE BROTH
(PAGE 87)

René Verdon

In the 1960s, René Verdon was the White House chef under Presidents Kennedy and Johnson. He subsequently settled in San Francisco, where he operated Le Trianon restaurant from 1972 to 1986. He has written four cookbooks, *The White House Chef* (Doubleday, 1967), *French Cooking for the American Table* (Doubleday, 1974), *The Enlightened Cuisine* (Macmillan, 1985) and *Convection Cuisine* (Morrow, 1988).

SCALLOPS, ROMA TOMATOES, AND SNOW PEAS WITH
TARRAGON AND GARLIC OIL (PAGE 49)

Andy Wai

Andy Wai was born in Hong Kong, where he started cooking at age fifteen. He apprenticed in various seafood houses, and spent four years in the upscale restaurant of Hong Kong's Miramar Hotel. In 1986, he started working for the Harbor Village restaurant in Hong Kong, and was sent to San Francisco in 1988 for the opening of a new Harbor Village in the Embarcadero Center. He became the executive chef of the Cantonese-style seafood restaurant in 1991.

TWOFOLD PROSPERITY CLAMS (PAGE 62)
SPICY TOFU WITH LINGUINE (PAGE 88)

Maggie Waldron

Maggie Waldron is senior vice-president of Ketchum Communications in San Francisco and executive creative director of the Ketchum Food Center, which specializes in the marketing of fresh fruit and vegetables. A former magazine editor and television director, she is the author of several cookbooks, including *Barbecue & Smoke Cookery* (101 Productions, 1983) and *Cold Spaghetti at Midnight* (Morrow, 1992).

UDON SUKI (PAGE 89)

Alice Waters

Alice Waters is the founding chef and proprietor of Berkeley's renowned Chez Panisse restaurant and its upstairs café, which opened in 1971 and 1980 respectively. In 1984, she opened Cafe Fanny, also in Berkeley. Her publications include *Chez Panisse Menu Cookbook* (Random House, 1982), *Chez Panisse Cooking*, written with Paul Bertolli (Random House, 1988) and *Fanny at Chez Panisse* (HarperCollins, 1992).

SALMON POACHED IN COURT BOUILLON WITH
SALSA VERDE (PAGE 108)

Kirk Webber

Kirk Webber began cooking in his father's restaurant in Orange County, California, while he was still in high school. After graduating from the California Culinary Academy in San Francisco, he worked in various restaurants, including the City Restaurant in Los Angeles. Since 1990, he has been the chef-proprietor of Cafe Kati, in San Francisco.

THAI-STYLE PRAWN CAKES (PAGE 59)
SEA BASS BAKED IN PARCHMENT WITH
LEMON AND THYME (PAGE 100)

Frances Wilson

Frances Wilson is a native of Dublin, Ireland, who studied cooking at the Dublin College of Catering. She taught high school home economics until 1990, when she took a year's leave of absence and, enticed by the California food scene, came to Berkeley. She found work in Haig Krikorian's esteemed Lalime's restaurant and decided not to return to teaching. She became the executive chef in 1993.

SWISS CHARD LEAVES FILLED WITH MUSHROOMS AND ASPARAGUS WITH ROASTED TOMATO SAUCE (PAGE 46)
HALIBUT STUFFED WITH SCALLOP MOUSSE WITH SPICY ORANGE-GINGER SAUCE (PAGE 104)

Martin Yan

Martin Yan is a popular television host and Chinese chef who has over 700 half-hour cooking shows to his credit. His PBS series, *Yan Can Cook*, emanates from KQED in San Francisco, airs on 245 stations across the United States and is broadcast abroad in 50 countries. He has written seven cookbooks, including *The Joy of Wokking* (Doubleday, 1979), *Yan Can Cook* (Doubleday, 1981), *Martin Yan, the Chinese Chef* (Doubleday, 1985), *A Wok for All Seasons* (Doubleday, 1988), *Everybody's Wokking* (Harlow & Ratner, 1991), *The Well-Seasoned Wok* (Harlow & Ratner, 1993) and *A Simple Guide to Chinese Ingredients and Other Asian Specialties* (Yan Can Cook, Inc. 1994).

CORN AND SHELLFISH SOUP (PAGE 41)
MY UNCLE'S POACHED FISH (PAGE 111)

Walter Zolezzi

Walter Zolezzi is a native San Franciscan who had a long career in the wholesale food business prior to opening his first restaurant, the Fly Trap, in 1989. He named it after a defunct but fondly remembered downtown fish and chop house, and carried on the tradition of the old Fly Trap with updated recipes of early San Francisco. Before he became a chef, Zolezzi worked in his family's poultry and seafood processing company, which he continued to run after it was sold to Del Monte in 1967. He retired in 1985 to raise Arabian horses at his ranch near Santa Rosa, but got back into harness for the Fly Trap, which he operates with managing partner Glenn Meyers and chef de cuisine Robby Morgenstein.

RISOTTO WITH WILD MUSHROOMS AND BABY ARTICHOKES (PAGE 89)

soups

Beet Soup with Ginger and Chive Cream
Gloria Ciccarone-Nehls

Chinese Spicy Soup
Marion Cunningham

Chilled Golden Bell Pepper Soup
Barbara Figueroa

Curried Broccoli Soup
Joyce Goldstein

Butternut and Acorn Squash Soup
Charles Saunders

**Red Miso Soup with Soba Noodles
and Shiitake Mushrooms**
Julie Ann Ring

Gazpacho with Crabmeat
Wolfgang Puck

Corn and Shellfish Soup
Martin Yan

Sopa Ranchera
Reed Hearon

Beet Soup with Ginger and Chive Cream
Gloria Ciccarone-Nehls

I conceived this soup when I was working in England at the Chester Grosvenor Hotel. I had agreed to appear on a TV cooking show called *The Seven-Pound Challenge*, where I had to make a four-course meal for four persons for seven pounds (about eleven dollars). Needless to say, beets were one of my options, due to the low price. For good measure, the soup is also very low in fat.

1 tablespoon olive oil
2 cloves garlic, minced
1- to 2-inch piece of fresh ginger, peeled and minced
1 medium-size yellow onion, thinly sliced
1 large potato, peeled and thinly sliced
6 large beets, peeled and thinly sliced
Juice of 1 to 2 lemons
1/4 cup red wine vinegar
8 cups chicken stock (page 147) or canned fat-free,
    low-salt chicken broth
Salt and white pepper to taste
2 bunches fresh chives
1 cup low-fat sour cream or plain yogurt

In a 4-quart nonreactive saucepan, heat the olive oil and sauté the garlic, ginger and onion over medium heat until soft, about 5 minutes. Add the potato and beets and continue to sauté for another minute. Add the juice of 1 lemon, the vinegar, and chicken stock. Bring to a boil. Reduce heat and simmer until beets are soft, 45 minutes to 1 hour. Season with salt and pepper to taste.

Let mixture cool a little, pour into a blender in batches and purée until very smooth. Taste to correct seasoning, and, if you think it's necessary, add more lemon juice. Set aside.

Cut 2-inch tips from the chives and reserve for garnish. Blanch the stalks of the chives in boiling salted water for 2 minutes. Purée in a blender with just enough water to make a smooth, firm purée. In a bowl, fold chives into the sour cream or yogurt, season with salt and pepper, and mix well. Cover and refrigerate if not serving immediately.

When ready to serve, gently reheat the soup and ladle into warm bowls. Garnish each bowl with a dollop of chive cream and 2 snipped chives. The soup may also be served chilled.

Yield: ten 1 1/3 -cup servings.
Per serving: 94 calories, 6 g protein, 11 g carbohydrates, 3 g fat (.7 g saturated), 1 mg cholesterol, 653 mg sodium.

Chinese Spicy Soup
Marion Cunningham

Here is a light and spicy soup everyone will ask for after they've tasted it. I made it for M.F.K. Fisher and she immediately asked for the recipe. She told me afterward that it became one of her favorite dishes. Serve it with warm flour tortillas spread with Chinese plum sauce and sprinkled with sliced scallions.

6 cups chicken stock (page 147) or canned fat-free,
    low-salt chicken broth
4 ounces fresh mushrooms, sliced
4 ounces (1 1/2 cups packed) spinach, well washed
3 tablespoons low-sodium soy sauce
3 tablespoons cider vinegar
3/4 teaspoon freshly ground pepper
2 1/4 teaspoons Asian sesame oil
1/2 teaspoon Asian hot chili oil or Tabasco sauce (taste the
    soup before adding the full amount)
12 ounces firm tofu, cut into small dice
3 tablespoons cornstarch dissolved in 5 tablespoons water
1 egg, beaten
3 tablespoons finely chopped fresh cilantro
2 scallions, finely chopped

Put the chicken stock, mushrooms and spinach in a large saucepan. Bring to a boil, lower heat and simmer for 4 minutes.

Mix together the soy sauce, vinegar, pepper, sesame oil and hot chili oil in a small bowl. Stir until well blended, then add to the broth. Taste and correct the seasonings.

Add the tofu and the cornstarch to the broth, stirring constantly until the soup thickens. Pour the beaten egg into the simmering broth and continue to stir until the egg forms ribbons. Add the cilantro and scallions and serve at once.

Yield: six 1 ¹/₃-cup servings.
Per serving: 137 calories, 11 g protein, 8 g carbohydrates, 6 g fat (1 g saturated), 35 mg cholesterol, 785 mg sodium.

CHILLED GOLDEN BELL PEPPER SOUP
Barbara Figueroa

This soup, with its warm, sunny color, delivers a whole range of flavors and textures. Smooth, creamy and crunchy elements all coexist in a single bowl. A cool, refreshing initial taste, replete with citrus, sweet peppers and cilantro, makes way for the tingle of smoky chilies.

4 medium-size yellow bell peppers
4 medium-size red bell peppers
2 cups fresh corn kernels (scraped from about 3 ears of corn)
2 tablespoons olive oil
3 shallots, chopped
3 cloves garlic, chopped
1 tablespoon chili powder
1 tablespoon ground cumin
6 cups chicken stock (page 147) or canned fat-free, low-salt chicken broth
1 ¹/₂ ancho chilies, seeded and chopped
1 ¹/₂ cups fresh orange juice
1 ³/₄ cups nonfat plain yogurt
Salt and freshly ground pepper to taste
¹/₂ cup chopped fresh cilantro
Fresh cilantro sprigs for garnish

Cut the yellow and red peppers into quarters. Remove seeds, stems and ribs. Cut quarters into 3 or 4 pieces.

In a large saucepan of boiling water, blanch the corn kernels for 2 minutes. Remove, drain and chill. Set aside.

In a large saucepan or soup pot, heat the olive oil and gently sauté the shallots and garlic over medium heat until translucent, about 2 minutes. Add the chili powder and cumin. Cook, stirring, over low heat for 1 or 2 minutes. Do not allow to burn. Add the chicken stock, ancho chilies and bell peppers. Cover and simmer for 25 to 30 minutes, until the peppers are soft.

Purée mixture in batches in a blender. Strain through a medium fine sieve into a large bowl. Place bowl in a large container of ice to cool, stirring frequently. When soup is cold, whisk in the orange juice and 1 ¹/₂ cups of the yogurt. Season with salt and pepper as needed.

To serve, ladle soup into 12 bowls. To each bowl, add about ¹/₄ cup corn kernels (be generous) and 2 teaspoons chopped cilantro. Stir together. Top each with a dollop of the remaining yogurt and a sprig of cilantro.

Yield: twelve 1 ¹/₄ cup servings.
Per serving: 130 calories, 6 g protein, 19 g carbohydrates, 3 g fat (.6 g saturated), .5 mg cholesterol, 517 mg sodium.

CURRIED BROCCOLI SOUP
Joyce Goldstein

Apple and potato cut the cabbagy taste of the broccoli, making a rich, full-flavored soup that even a confirmed broccoli-phobe like George Bush might like.

*5 cups chicken stock (page 147) or canned fat-free, low-salt
  chicken broth*
1 yellow onion, diced (about 1 1/2 cups)
1 tart green apple, peeled and sliced
1 small potato, peeled and thinly sliced
3 cups chopped broccoli (about 1 pound)
1 tablespoon curry powder
1 teaspoon ground ginger
1 cup nonfat plain yogurt
Salt and freshly ground pepper to taste
Lemon slices or chopped mint leaves for garnish

In a large saucepan, bring 2 cups of the stock to a boil. Add the onion and simmer over medium heat until the onion is translucent, about 10 minutes. Add the apple and potato and cook until tender, about 20 minutes. Add the broccoli, curry, ginger and the remaining 3 cups of stock. Simmer until broccoli is tender, about 10 minutes. Purée the soup in batches in a blender. Whisk in the yogurt and adjust seasoning with salt and pepper. To serve, garnish with lemon slices or chopped mint leaves. The soup is good hot or cold.

Yield: six 1 1/3-cup servings.
Per serving: 132 calories, 9 g protein, 20 g carbohydrates, 1 g fat (.5 g saturated), .6 mg cholesterol, 614 mg sodium.

BUTTERNUT AND ACORN SQUASH SOUP
Charles Saunders

When fashioning a dish for the Eastside Oyster Bar & Grill, my restaurant in Sonoma, I feel that four essential factors must be present—color, flavor, texture and harmony. This butternut and acorn squash soup combines all four in a fall spectrum. The soup is high in flavor and low in fat, and it's great to serve with a skillet cornbread when the weather turns chilly and drizzle is forecast.

1 medium-size butternut squash (about 1 1/4 pounds)
2 medium-size acorn squash (about 1 pound each)
Salt and freshly ground pepper to taste
1 medium-size yellow onion, thinly sliced
1 stalk celery, thinly and diagonally sliced
1 Granny Smith apple, unpeeled, cored and thinly sliced
*5 cups vegetable stock (page 148), chicken stock
  (page 147) or water*
1 teaspoon curry powder
1/2 teaspoon ground cumin
1/2 teaspoon Chinese five-spice powder
6 cloves garlic, roasted (page 149)
*Chopped fresh parsley, chopped fresh sage and toasted
  pumpkin seeds (page 150) for garnish*

Preheat the oven to 350 degrees F. Cut the 3 squash in half, leave in the seeds (they add flavor to the squash) and sprinkle the halves with salt and pepper. Place them seed side down on a baking sheet, pour in a cup of water and bake in the oven until tender, 45 minutes to 1 hour. Set aside to cool.

Place the onion, celery and apple in a steamer (or in a strainer placed in a large covered saucepan) and steam over boiling water until tender, 5 to 6 minutes. Remove to a baking sheet and set aside.

When the squash halves are cool enough to handle, remove the seeds and discard, and scoop out the flesh. Place flesh in a soup pot or large saucepan and add the water, vegetable or chicken stock. Bring to a boil, reduce heat and simmer for 10 minutes. Using a blender, purée the soup in batches, adding the curry, cumin, five-spice powder, roasted garlic, and salt and pepper.

Return the soup to the pot and add the steamed onion, celery and apple. Reheat to a simmer. Serve each bowl garnished with chopped parsley, sage and toasted pumpkin seeds.

Yield: eight 1 1/4 cup servings.
Per serving: 137 calories, 4 g protein, 30 g carbohydrates, 1 g fat (.2 g saturated), 0 mg cholesterol, 400 mg sodium.

RED MISO SOUP WITH SOBA NOODLES AND SHIITAKE MUSHROOMS
Julie Ann Ring

This Japanese-accented soup is a very good fast-food favorite of mine. Because miso is made from soybeans and soba noodles from buckwheat, the soup is flavorful, low in fat and high in protein. The ingredients may not sound familiar, but are readily available in Asian markets or your local supermarket. They're the kind of ingredients that you can keep on your kitchen shelf indefinitely, making this dish a spur-of-the-moment delight. Serve it for lunch or a late-night supper. For a side dish, you may want to offer a cucumber and tomato salad with fresh lime juice.

VEGETABLE BROTH
1 large yellow onion, cut up
2 carrots, sliced
2 stalks celery, sliced
1 leek, white part only, well washed and sliced
3 cloves garlic, mashed
6 cups water

2 tablespoons red miso (soybean) paste
Salt and freshly ground pepper to taste
4 ounces soba (Japanese buckwheat) noodles
1 tablespoon peanut oil
3 cloves garlic, minced
8 ounces fresh shiitake mushrooms, cut into julienne strips
1 teaspoon grated fresh ginger
Toasted sesame seeds (page 150) and finely sliced scallions
  for garnish

Prepare the vegetable broth in a large saucepan, combining the ingredients with the water. Bring to a boil. Reduce heat, cover and simmer over low heat for 1 hour. Strain, discarding vegetables, and return broth to the pan.

Bring vegetable broth back to a boil. In a small bowl, dilute the red miso paste with a cup of hot vegetable broth, stirring to cream the miso. Add the creamed miso to the pan of vegetable broth. Season with salt, if needed, and pepper. Keep warm.

Drop the soba noodles into a large saucepan of boiling water, and cook over medium heat until al dente, about 6 minutes. Drain in a colander, run under cold water to stop the cooking, and set aside.

Coat a skillet with the peanut oil and heat over medium heat. Add the garlic, mushrooms and ginger, and season lightly with salt and pepper. Cook until the mushrooms are tender, about 5 minutes.

To serve, divide the mushrooms and noodles among 4 soup bowls and ladle in vegetable broth. Top with sesame seeds and sliced scallions. Serve with chopsticks as well as a soup spoon.

Yield: four 1 3/4 -cup servings.
Per serving: 148 calories, 4 g protein, 17 g carbohydrates, 3 g fat (.5 g saturated), 0 mg cholesterol, 383 mg sodium.

Gazpacho with Crabmeat
Wolfgang Puck

Gazpacho is a refreshing and healthy beginning to a warm-weather meal. Family or friends, vegetarian or not, will welcome this deliciously simple way to get your daily vitamin supply. This untraditional version, in which crabmeat is added to the chilled vegetable soup, has been a favorite with customers at Spago and Postrio. To achieve the right texture this recipe requires a food processor—not a blender.

2 1/2 pounds (7 or 8) medium-size, very ripe tomatoes, cored
  and quartered
2 medium-size cucumbers, peeled and seeded
1 medium-size red, yellow or green bell pepper, cored, seeded
  and cut into 1-inch chunks
2 large stalks celery, cut into 1-inch pieces
3 tablespoons tomato paste
Salt to taste
1/2 teaspoon freshly ground pepper
1/2 teaspoon cayenne pepper
3 tablespoons olive oil
1 tablespoon sherry vinegar
2 cups vegetable stock (page 148) or tomato juice
8 ounces cooked lump crabmeat (cooked lobster or shrimp
  may be substituted)

In a large, nonreactive bowl, combine the tomatoes, 1 1/2 cucumbers, bell pepper, celery, tomato paste, salt, pepper and cayenne. Pour the olive oil and vinegar over the mixture, cover and refrigerate 6 to 8 hours, or overnight, stirring occasionally.

Using a food processor, process the chilled mixture until the vegetables are minced but still retain some texture. (This will have to be done in 2 or 3 batches.) Return to bowl and pour in the stock or tomato juice. Correct seasoning to taste and chill until serving time.

When ready to serve, cut the remaining 1/2 cucumber into thin slices. Ladle the gazpacho into 8 soup bowls. Garnish with the cucumber slices and top with the crabmeat.

Yield: eight 1 1/3 -cup servings.
Per serving: 119 calories, 7 g protein, 13 g carbohydrates, 4 g fat (.6 g saturated), 18 mg cholesterol, 360 mg sodium.

Corn and Shellfish Soup
Martin Yan

Yes, China has corn. (Where do you think cornstarch comes from?) One favorite Chinese way to use sweet corn is in luscious seafood soups. This version uses scallops and crabmeat, but feel free to use all scallops, or any other shellfish combination you like.

4 dried Chinese black or shiitake mushrooms
6 cups chicken stock (page 147) or canned fat-free,
  low-salt chicken broth
2 teaspoons slivered fresh ginger
1 can (about 1 pound) cream-style corn
4 ounces bay scallops
4 ounces cooked crabmeat, flaked
1/2 cup frozen peas, thawed
1 teaspoon Asian sesame oil
Salt and white pepper to taste
4 teaspoons cornstarch dissolved in 2 tablespoons water
1 egg white

Soak the mushrooms in a bowl of warm water to cover for 30 minutes. Drain. Cut off and discard the stems. Thinly slice the caps. Set aside.

In a large saucepan, bring the chicken stock, ginger and mushrooms to a boil over high heat. Reduce the heat, add the corn, scallops, crabmeat and peas, and cook over medium heat until the scallops turn opaque, about 1 minute. Stir in the sesame oil, salt and pepper. Add the cornstarch solution and cook, stirring, until the soup boils and thickens,

about 1 minute. Lightly beat the egg white in a bowl. Remove the pan from the heat and slowly drizzle in the egg white, stirring constantly, to form "egg flowers."

Yield: six 1 ¹/₄ -cup servings.
Per serving: 164 calories, 15 g protein, 20 g carbohydrates, 3 g fat (.6 saturated), 20 mg cholesterol, 810 mg sodium.

Sopa Ranchera
Reed Hearon

This is a ranch-country Mexican soup, the sort that's so simple to make, it might almost be thrown together with leftovers in the kitchen. I first came across it at a friend's house in Oaxaca, and was struck at the time by the wonderfully bright, clean flavors. We've served it on a regular basis at the Café Marimba since we opened the restaurant. People like to order it because it's hearty enough to make a great lunch or light supper all by itself. Be sure to use Mexican oregano (available at Latin markets), not the Italian variety. The flavor is quite different.

6 cups chicken stock (page 147) or canned fat-free, low-salt chicken broth
2 boneless and skinless whole chicken breasts, cut into julienne strips
1 cup cooked white rice
Bouquet garni of 1 teaspoon dried Mexican oregano, 2 whole cloves and 1 teaspoon black peppercorns, tied in cheesecloth
4 to 6 jalapeño chilies, chopped with seeds
1 cup peeled, seeded and diced ripe tomatoes
¹/₂ white onion, chopped
1 medium-size ripe avocado, peeled and diced
3 tablespoons chopped fresh cilantro
Salt and freshly ground pepper to taste
4 limes

In a large saucepan or stockpot, bring the chicken stock to a boil, reduce the heat, add the julienned chicken breasts, rice and bouquet garni, and poach at a simmer over low heat for 10 minutes.

Add the jalapeños, tomatoes, onion, avocado and cilantro to the soup, bring back to a boil, stir, and cook for just 1 minute. Remove the bouquet garni and season with salt and pepper. Ladle the hot soup into 8 bowls and squeeze the juice of ¹/₂ lime into each bowl.

Yield: eight 1 ¹/₃ -cup servings.
Per serving: 261 calories, 31 g protein, 15 g carbohydrates, 8 g fat (1.7 g saturated), 72 mg cholesterol, 608 mg sodium.

3

appetizers and light entrées

Swiss Chard Leaves Filled with Mushrooms and Asparagus with Roasted Tomato Sauce
Frances Wilson

Amelio's Vegetable Pâté
Jacky Robert

Artichoke Stuffed with Pine Nuts and Currants with Meyer Lemon Vinaigrette
Margie Conard and Dana Tommasino

Tuna Tartare on Nori Rounds
Elka Gilmore

Scallops, Roma Tomatoes and Snow Peas with Tarragon and Garlic Oil
René Verdon

Grilled Scallops with Lentils, Piperade and Balsamic Syrup
Amey Shaw

Fish Paillard with Ginger, Garlic and Tomatoes
Jeremiah Tower

Seafood Mosaic with Cranberry Syrup, Watercress Coulis and Beet-Fennel Salad
Peter DeMarais

Hot and Sour Squid
Barbara Tropp

An East-Meets-West Sandwich
Ken Hom

Sardines with Fennel, Sweet Onion, Raisins and Sun-Dried Tomato
Mary Etta Moose

Grilled Prawns with Papaya Salsa
Paula LeDuc

Tandoori-Style Barbecued Prawns over Mixed Greens
Irene Trias

Thai-Style Prawn Cakes
Kirk Webber

Mandarin Quail with Ginger Juice and Cinnamon Oil
Ercolino Crugnale

Twofold Prosperity Clams
Andy Wai

Turkey Chili with Tomatillos
Kelly Mills

Flat Bread Tostada with Black Beans, Poached Egg and Tomatillo Salsa
Cindy Pawlcyn

Tofu-Vegetable Scramble
Margaret Fox

Stir-Fried Garlic Chicken with Cilantro
Anne and David Gingrass

Swiss Chard Leaves Filled with Mushrooms and Asparagus with Roasted Tomato Sauce

Frances Wilson

We offer this dish at Lalime's as an appetizer, with two filled chard leaves per serving. But it also lends itself to serving as a dinner entrée, with three leaves apiece, accompanied with spiced couscous or risotto. The roasted tomato sauce has become a classic at Lalime's. The roasting of the tomatoes gives the sauce a deeper, richer taste. The herbs for the sauce can vary with the season. Instead of thyme, you can use basil or oregano for a different flavor.

Roasted Tomato Sauce

4 pounds large ripe tomatoes
2 tablespoons olive oil
Salt and freshly ground pepper to taste
1 yellow onion, finely chopped
1 large carrot, finely chopped
2 stalks celery, finely chopped
2 cloves garlic, finely chopped
2 teaspoons ground cumin
1 teaspoon paprika
1 bay leaf
1 tablespoon chopped fresh thyme
Salt and freshly ground pepper to taste

Mushroom-Asparagus Filling

*1 pound asparagus, trimmed and cut diagonally
    into 1-inch pieces*
6 scallions, finely chopped
2 tablespoons chopped fresh oregano
15 ounces low-fat ricotta cheese
1 tablespoon olive oil
1 pound fresh mushrooms, sliced
3 cloves garlic, finely chopped
Salt and freshly ground pepper to taste

1 bunch red Swiss chard (about 1 pound)

To prepare the sauce, preheat the oven to 500 degrees F. Remove the stems from the tomatoes, and with a paring knife, cut an X on the bottom of each tomato. Place them on a baking sheet, brush with 1 tablespoon of the olive oil, sprinkle with salt and pepper, and roast in the oven until soft to the touch, about 20 minutes.

Meanwhile, heat 1 tablespoon olive oil in a medium-size, heavy-bottomed, nonreactive saucepan and add the onion, carrot, celery and garlic. Cook over low heat until the onion is translucent, about 2 minutes. Add the cumin, paprika, bay leaf and thyme and continue to cook for 5 minutes.

When the tomatoes are finished roasting, allow them to cool slightly and pass them through a sieve or food mill. Add the sieved tomatoes to the vegetable mixture in the saucepan and bring to a boil. Turn heat to low and gently simmer for at least 30 minutes. The longer it cooks the richer the sauce. Season with salt and pepper. The sauce can be made in advance and reheated when needed.

To prepare the filling, blanch the asparagus pieces in a saucepan of boiling water over medium heat for 1 or 2 minutes. Drain and transfer to a large bowl. Add the scallions, oregano and ricotta cheese. Set aside.

Heat the olive oil in a medium-size skillet over medium heat and sauté the mushrooms and garlic until golden brown, about 5 minutes. Combine with the other filling ingredients and mix well. Season with salt and pepper.

Select 12 large, unblemished chard leaves from the bunch. Wash well and remove the thick stems. Blanch the leaves in a large saucepan of boiling water over medium heat for 2 minutes. Remove and drain well on paper towels.

Spread the leaves out flat on a work surface and place a heaping teaspoonful of filling in the center of each leaf. Fold the sides inward over the filling and then roll the leaf up, making a little parcel. Repeat with each leaf. (If a leaf is too small, overlap two leaves.) Place filled leaves on a platter, cover with plastic wrap and store in refrigerator until needed.

Just before serving, bring water to a boil in a steamer (or in a large covered saucepan fitted with a rack), lay a few filled leaves at a time on the rack and steam for 10 minutes, until they are heated through. Serve 2 leaves per person as an appetizer on warm plates surrounded by heated tomato sauce.

Yield: 6 servings.
Per serving: 254 calories, 19 g protein, 34 g carbohydrates, 6 g fat (.9 g saturated), 0 mg cholesterol, 437 g sodium.

AMELIO'S VEGETABLE PÂTÉ
Jacky Robert

I developed this vegetable pâté as a summer appetizer soon after I took over Amelio's in 1985, and brought my own French cooking style to a landmark Italian restaurant in San Francisco's North Beach district. Since I wanted to pay homage to the wonderful Italian food of my North Beach neighbors, I made this dish with a base of ripe tomatoes, served it with slices of fresh mozzarella and prosciutto, and drizzled basil oil over the pâté slices. My original recipe was made with cream. This updated version conforms to today's health standards in being very low in fat. In place of cream, I use egg whites and nonfat yogurt.

2 small carrots, cut into ¼ -inch sticks
2 cups broccoli florets
2 cups cauliflower florets
2 large asparagus
6 string beans
1 medium-size zucchini, cut into ¼ -inch sticks
1 small yellow onion, sliced
1 tablespoon olive oil
10 large, ripe tomatoes, quartered
2 cloves garlic, chopped
Bouquet garni of 2 sprigs fresh thyme, 3 sprigs fresh parsley
   and 2 bay leaves, tied in cheesecloth
Salt and cayenne pepper to taste
1 tablespoon (1 envelope) unflavored gelatin
¼ cup cold water
2 egg whites
½ cup nonfat plain yogurt
Basil oil (page 149) for garnish
Thinly sliced prosciutto and mozzarella cheese
   (optional) for garnish

In a medium-size saucepan, blanch the carrots, broccoli, cauliflower, asparagus, string beans and zucchini separately in salted boiling water until al dente, about 2 to 4 minutes for each vegetable. Refresh them in a bowl of ice water, drain them and pat them dry with a towel. Set aside.

In a heavy-bottomed, medium-size nonreactive saucepan, sweat the onion in the olive oil over medium heat until translucent, about 5 minutes. Add the tomatoes, garlic and bouquet garni. Cook over medium heat for about 30 minutes, until the juices have evaporated and only 2 cups of the mixture remain. Remove and discard the bouquet garni. Purée the mixture in a blender and strain through a fine sieve into a medium-size bowl. Season with salt and cayenne.

In a small saucepan, soften the gelatin in ¼ cup cold water, then heat over low heat for 1 to 2 minutes until the gelatin is dissolved. Add the warm gelatin to the tomato mixture and mix well with a whisk. Place the bowl in a large bowl of ice and continue whisking while cooling the mixture. In another medium-size bowl, whip the egg whites to soft peaks and fold into the tomato mixture. Fold in the yogurt.

Assemble the pâté in a rectangular 2-quart terrine mold lined with plastic wrap. Lay in the different vegetables a layer at a time, spooning some tomato mixture over each layer, until no vegetables remain. Cover terrine with plastic wrap and hit it several times on the work surface to eliminate any air bubbles between vegetables.

Refrigerate for 2 hours. Unmold, cut into thick slices and serve drizzled with basil oil, or, if you wish, garnished with thin slices of prosciutto and fresh mozzarella.

Yield: 10 servings.
Per serving: 89 calories, 4 g protein, 12 g carbohydrates, 3 g fat (.4 g saturated), .2 mg cholesterol, 145 mg sodium.

ARTICHOKE STUFFED WITH PINE NUTS AND CURRANTS WITH MEYER LEMON VINAIGRETTE
Margie Conard and Dana Tommasino

We think this stuffed artichoke nicely represents the style of food we serve at Woodward's Garden. It is seasonal, unfussy and tasty, yet the flavors work well together and stand out individually. It's a great first-course appetizer, or the artichokes can be quartered and passed as an hors d'oeuvre.

4 large artichokes (about 10 ounces each)

PINE NUT-CURRANT STUFFING
1/2 cup bread crumbs
3 tablespoons dried currants
3 tablespoons toasted pine nuts (page 150)
1 tablespoon freshly grated Parmesan cheese
1 tablespoon chopped fresh parsley
1 tablespoon olive oil
Salt and freshly ground pepper to taste

MEYER LEMON VINAIGRETTE
2 tablespoons finely chopped shallots
2 tablespoons fresh Meyer lemon juice
3 tablespoons champagne vinegar
2 tablespoons olive oil
Salt and freshly ground pepper to taste

Cut off stems of artichokes. Slice 1/2 inch off tops and snip off tips of leaves. Place the artichokes in a large saucepan of boiling water, lower heat and cook at a simmer until tender, about 25 minutes. When done, the stem end should yield to the point of a small knife. Drain and let cool. When artichokes are cool enough to handle, scoop out the chokes with a large spoon. Set aside.

To prepare the stuffing, in a small bowl, combine all the ingredients. Mix well and set aside.

To prepare the vinaigrette, in a small bowl, whisk together the shallots, lemon juice and vinegar. Add the olive oil, season to taste with salt and pepper, and whisk well. Set aside.

To stuff the artichokes, gently pull back the leaves and drop some stuffing in the cavity and between the leaves. Do not overstuff. Place the artichokes in an ovenproof skillet or baking pan.

When ready to serve, preheat the oven to 400 degrees F. Place the artichokes in the oven until bread crumbs are brown, 5 to 7 minutes. Serve immediately with a drizzle of vinaigrette.

Yield: 4 servings.
Per serving: 273 calories, 10 g protein, 31 g carbohydrates, 11 g fat (2 g saturated), 1 mg cholesterol, 504 mg sodium

Tuna Tartare on Nori Rounds
Elka Gilmore

Here is a modern interpretation of the classic steak tartare, with ahi tuna substituting for ground red meat. As in the original dish, the tuna is brightly seasoned and eaten raw. Be certain to obtain very fresh, top quality tuna, like the sushi tuna sold in Japanese markets. Most of the Asian ingredients in this recipe are available at better supermarkets. If you can't find the nori, use an easier method and serve the tuna atop cucumber slices.

Tuna Tartare
*1/2 pound number-one grade ahi tuna, cut into
    1/4-inch dice*
2 tablespoons peeled, seeded and finely chopped cucumber
2 tablespoons finely chopped scallions
1 teaspoon grated fresh ginger
1 teaspoon mirin (Japanese sweet rice wine)
1/2 teaspoon Asian sesame oil
Salt and freshly ground pepper to taste

Nori Rounds
1 cup cooked sushi rice (page 150)
1 teaspoon rice vinegar
2 sheets nori (Japanese dried seaweed)
Bamboo sushi mat (a tea towel can be substituted)
1/2 teaspoon wasabi (Japanese horseradish)

Daikon radish sprouts for garnish

In a small bowl, mix together the tuna tartare ingredients, and keep chilled until ready to use.

To prepare nori rounds, sprinkle the sushi rice with vinegar and mix. Lightly toast nori sheets over a gas flame, 1 minute each. Lay a nori sheet on a bamboo sushi mat and spread evenly with half the rice, leaving 1/2 inch uncovered on each end. Spread half the wasabi down the center of the rice. Roll to 1-inch diameter and cut into 1/2-inch rounds. Repeat process with second nori sheet. You should have about 16 nori rounds.

Mound the tuna tartare on nori rounds. Garnish with daikon sprouts and serve immediately.

Yield: 4 servings.
Per serving: 182 calories, 1.5 g protein, 19 g carbohydrates, 4 g fat (.9 g saturated), 21 mg cholesterol, 163 mg sodium.

Scallops, Roma Tomatoes and Snow Peas with Tarragon and Garlic Oil
René Verdon

More often than not, the pressure of a deadline helps an idea germinate and blossom. This is the case with the following recipe, which I worked out with my friend Christian Clanet for a dinner he gave for me and my wife. He hadn't given much thought to the appetizer until the day of the event. He phoned me to say that he wanted to do a light dish with scallops and Roma tomatoes, and that he thought the final phase of the preparation should take no more than four or five minutes so he would not spend too much time in the kitchen away from his guests. I gave him some guidelines, and I'm pleased to present to you this low-fat and tasty appetizer. For a main course, double the recipe. You can also substitute prawns or steamed whitefish for the scallops.

3 tablespoons olive oil, plus more for sautéing
1 clove garlic, finely sliced
8 fresh tarragon leaves, chopped
20 medium-size Roma (plum) tomatoes
Powdered sugar for dusting tomatoes
20 snow peas
20 sea scallops (about 1 pound)
Salt and freshly ground pepper to taste
1/2 lime

Place 1 ½ tablespoons olive oil in each of 2 containers and marinate the garlic and tarragon separately, from 6 to 24 hours.

Preheat the oven to 275 degrees F. Cut a small piece off the stem end of the tomatoes to let the juice escape and evaporate during baking. Place the tomatoes on the rack of a broiler pan so the liquid can drop through, and bake in the oven for about 4 hours, until they look like sun-dried tomatoes. You can also use a roasting pan for the tomatoes and spoon off the liquid as often as necessary. Lightly dust the tomatoes with sugar ½ hour before they're done baking. The tomatoes can be prepared a day ahead and reheated in a 300-degree F oven for 5 minutes before serving.

Steam the snow peas for 5 minutes in a steamer or small covered saucepan with ½ cup simmering water.

In a nonstick skillet rubbed with a little olive oil, sauté the scallops over high heat for 1 ½ minutes on each side. Remove from heat, season with salt and pepper, and squeeze lime juice over the scallops, rolling them around to distribute the flavor.

Serve as an appetizer on warm plates, placing tomatoes in a circle in the center of the plate. Place a drop of garlic oil on each tomato. Arrange the scallops at the edge of the tomatoes. Place a drop of tarragon oil on each scallop. Put a warm snow pea between each scallop.

Yield: 4 servings.
Per serving: 223 calories, 22 g protein, 16 g carbohydrates, 8 g fat (1 g saturated), 37 mg cholesterol, 201 mg sodium.

GRILLED SCALLOPS WITH LENTILS, PIPERADE AND BALSAMIC SYRUP
Amey Shaw

The best scallops to use for this dish are called "day boat" sea scallops. These are harvested, shucked, packed dry and shipped within a day to their destination. The flavor is sweeter, the texture more buttery and, because no chemicals or water are added to them, they tend to stick less to a cooking surface. Though this recipe may seem time consuming, it is simple to prepare. The lentils can be made a day ahead and kept refrigerated until an hour before serving. The piperade can be kept refrigerated for two days and warmed slightly before plating. The balsamic syrup can be stored at room temperature for a week. The French green lentils suggested for this recipe are smaller and more brightly flavored than the brown variety. They're available in better markets and specialty stores.

8 ounces French green lentils
1 medium-size carrot, cut into ⅛ -inch dice
½ medium-size yellow onion, cut into ⅛-inch dice
2 bay leaves
1 tablespoon cumin seeds, toasted and ground (page 150)
Kosher salt and freshly ground pepper to taste

PIPERADE
1 poblano chili, seeded and diced
1 medium-size yellow onion, diced
½ stalk celery, diced
*1 cup finely chopped fresh or canned Roma (plum) tomatoes
  with juice*
1 or 2 tablespoons Amey Shaw's spice mix (recipe follows)

4 cups good quality aged balsamic vinegar
12 large sea scallops (1 ounce each)
Vegetable oil spray
8 whole fresh chives for garnish

Wash lentils thoroughly. Drain and place in a 2-quart saucepan. Add carrots, onions, bay leaves, cumin, and salt and pepper to taste. Cover with cold water and bring to a boil. Turn down heat and cook at a simmer until lentils are al dente, about 25 minutes (or a bit more if you prefer creamier lentils). Drain off excess water and remove bay leaves. Set aside or keep warm in a double boiler.

To prepare the piperade, combine all the ingredients except spice mix in a nonreactive small saucepan. Season with spice mix, more or less to taste, reserving the remaining mix for another use. Cover pan and cook until the vegetables are soft, about 10 minutes. Remove from heat, let cool slightly, and purée in a blender. Set aside.

While the piperade is cooking, make the balsamic syrup. Place the vinegar in a medium-size, nonreactive saucepan and turn heat to medium high. Let boil until vinegar is reduced to about 1 cup. It should be the consistency of maple syrup. Let cool and transfer to a squeeze bottle.

To cook the scallops, preheat a grill or broiler. Pat dry the scallops, if needed, and lightly salt and pepper them. Spray the grill or broiler pan with vegetable oil spray. Place scallops on hot grill and cook for 1 to 2 minutes on each side for rare, or longer, if you wish.

Serve as an appetizer on 4 large warm plates. Place two heaping tablespoons of lentils in center of each. Place 3 separate teaspoons of piperade around the lentils, and lay a scallop on each piperade circle. Drizzle the balsamic syrup over the plate in a decorative pattern. Garnish each plate with 2 crisscrossed chives. To serve as an entrée, double the recipe.

Yield: 4 appetizer servings.
Per serving: 385 calories, 33 g protein, 65 g carbohydrates, 3 g fat (.3 g saturated), 28 mg cholesterol, 439 mg sodium.

AMEY SHAW'S SPICE MIX
1 teaspoon cayenne pepper
1 teaspoon freshly ground black pepper
1 teaspoon white pepper
1 teaspoon dried thyme
1 teaspoon garlic powder
1 teaspoon onion powder
2 tablespoons paprika
Kosher salt to taste

In a small bowl, mix together all the ingredients. Store in a tightly sealed container at room temperature.
Yield: 1/4 cup.

FISH PAILLARD WITH GINGER, GARLIC AND TOMATOES
Jeremiah Tower

Here is a low-fat version of a recipe I developed at the opening of my San Francisco restaurant, Stars, in 1984. I wanted a new, easily cooked and easily understood dish and it was an instant hit as an appetizer or lunch entrée. It can be with you at home, too. With a little advance chopping and slicing, you have a winner in five minutes. The original recipe used butter instead of olive oil, but the execution is essentially the same. The dish is so named because the fish is like a paillard of veal, cut very thin and pounded even thinner. It's so thin that you do not have to cook the fish in a pan. The heat of the plate and the heated sauce poured over the fish will do all the cooking.

4 fish fillets (such as halibut, sea bass, grouper, orange roughy, salmon, tuna, red snapper or sturgeon, 4 ounces each, no thicker than 1/3 inch)
2 teaspoons olive oil
Salt and freshly ground pepper to taste
1 cup fish stock (page 148)

2 ounces fresh ginger, peeled and finely chopped
3 cloves garlic, finely chopped
2 medium-size ripe tomatoes, peeled, seeded and diced
12 sprigs fresh cilantro

Preheat the broiler or oven to 400 degrees F. Pound the fish slices with the flat side of a large knife or cleaver until they are evenly ⅛ inch thick.

Spread the olive oil over 4 heat-resistant plates. Put the plates under the broiler or in the oven until they are very hot, about 2 minutes. Season the paillards with salt and pepper and put one on each hot plate.

Mix the fish stock, ginger, garlic and tomatoes in a medium-size skillet. Bring to a boil, season with salt and pepper and cook over medium-high heat for 3 minutes.

Turn the fish over on the plates and pour the sauce over the fish. By the time you garnish the plates with the cilantro, the fish will be done.

Yield: 4 servings.
Per serving: 188 calories, 26 g protein, 7 g carbohydrates, 5 g fat (.8 g saturated), 36 mg cholesterol, 532 mg sodium.

SEAFOOD MOSAIC WITH CRANBERRY SYRUP, WATERCRESS COULIS AND BEET-FENNEL SALAD
Peter DeMarais

I conceived this recipe for a seafood terrine for a cooking competition that took me to New York as a finalist to prepare the dish at James Beard House. I thought it up as a creative way to use seafood around the holidays. The dish is light, healthy, unusually tasty and looks very festive, especially with its two sauces, one green and the other red.

8 ounces squid
8 ounces crayfish tails or rock shrimp
8 ounces salmon fillet

COURT BOUILLON
1 teaspoon olive oil
⅓ cup chopped yellow onion
⅓ cup chopped carrot
⅓ cup chopped celery
1 sprig fresh thyme
4 sprigs fresh parsley
6 black peppercorns, crushed
2 whole cloves
½ bay leaf
2 tablespoons fresh lemon juice
¼ cup white wine
salt to taste
8 cups water

2 tablespoons (2 envelopes) unflavored gelatin
1 cup cold water
2 cups fish stock (page 148)
¼ cup Pernod
Salt to taste
1 tablespoon pink peppercorns
2 tablespoons chopped fresh dill
1 teaspoon chopped fresh thyme

CRANBERRY SYRUP
4 cups cranberry juice
2 cups fresh orange juice
1 cup cranberries
1 cup kumquats
1 tablespoon Grand Marnier
1 tablespoon canola oil

WATERCRESS COULIS

4 cups loosely packed, roughly chopped watercress with
stems (2 bunches)
2 cups loosely packed, roughly chopped parsley with
stems (1 bunch)
¼ cup fresh tarragon leaves
¼ cup fresh fennel sprigs
1 cup nonfat plain yogurt
Salt and freshly ground pepper to taste

BEET-FENNEL SALAD

1 pound beets, peeled
1 medium-size bulb fennel, cut into julienne strips
¼ cup fresh lemon juice
1 ½ tablespoons honey
2 tablespoons olive oil
Salt and freshly ground pepper to taste
Watercress sprigs for garnish

Clean and cut up fish into ¼-inch dice. Set aside.

Prepare the court bouillon: In a large, heavy-bottomed saucepan, heat the olive oil and sauté the onion, carrot and celery over medium heat without coloring for 5 minutes. Add remaining court bouillon ingredients, bring to a boil, reduce heat and simmer for 10 minutes. Strain and discard the solids.

Return the court bouillon to the saucepan, bring back to a boil over medium heat. Lower heat and blanch the fish at a simmer for 1 to 2 minutes, until medium rare. Remove and drain. Set aside.

In a small saucepan, soften gelatin in a cup of cold water, then heat over low heat, while stirring, until gelatin is dissolved. In a medium-size saucepan, bring the fish stock to a boil over medium heat and add the Pernod and salt. Pour in dissolved gelatin and whisk together.

In a large bowl, mix together the fish, peppercorns, dill and thyme, and season with salt. Line a rectangular 2-quart terrine mold with plastic wrap. Lay ⅓ of the fish mixture in bottom of terrine. Spoon ⅓ of the gelatin mixture over the fish. Wait 10 to 15 minutes until the gelatin has started to set, then repeat the procedure with another ⅓ of the fish and gelatin mixtures. If gelatin is no longer liquid, heat it gently to melt it. Wait again and repeat the procedure with remaining fish and gelatin. Refrigerate the terrine, covered with plastic wrap, until well chilled.

Prepare the cranberry syrup: In a medium-size saucepan, combine the cranberry and orange juices, bring to a boil, and simmer until reduced by half. Add the cranberries and kumquats, bring back to a boil, reduce heat and simmer for 5 minutes. Pass through a strainer, reserve the cranberries and kumquats and return juices to saucepan. Add the Grand Marnier and continue reducing the liquid until syrupy. Remove from heat and whisk in the oil. Set aside.

Prepare the watercress coulis: Place all the coulis ingredients in a blender and purée until smooth. Season with salt and pepper. Set aside.

Prepare the beet-fennel salad: Cook the beets in a saucepan of simmering water over medium heat until tender, about 8 minutes. Drain and cool. Cut beets into julienne strips. Set aside.

Blanch the fennel in a saucepan of simmering water over medium heat 1 to 2 minutes. Drain and cool.

In a large bowl, whisk together the lemon juice, honey, olive oil, salt and pepper. Just before serving, toss the fennel and beets with the vinaigrette. Do this at the last minute to keep the beets from bleeding into the fennel.

To serve, arrange on each plate a slice of seafood terrine, some fennel-beet salad and the contrasting cranberry and watercress sauces. Garnish with watercress sprigs and the reserved cranberries and sliced kumquats.

Yield: 10 servings.
Per serving: 572 calories, 22 g protein, 136 g carbohydrates, 8 g fat (1 g saturated), 83 mg cholesterol, 666 mg sodium.

Hot and Sour Squid
Barbara Tropp

Squid can be a grotesque affair to some people. First comes the cleaning, which some feel is like an episode out of a Stephen King novel. Then comes the cooking, which often yields tasteless rubber tires. I've no answer for the first problem since precleaned squid is typically salted or otherwise treated and not worthy of eating. But this dish is a fine remedy for the second. The squid is blanched no more than ten seconds, which leaves it velvety and fine, and is then tossed in a Hunanese mélange of spicy vegetables.

1 pound small squid (4 to 5 inches long and 1 inch wide)

AROMATICS
1 tablespoon finely minced fresh ginger
1 tablespoon finely minced garlic
*1 ½ tablespoons coarsely chopped Chinese fermented
   black beans*
2 tablespoons thinly sliced green and white scallion rings
¼ teaspoon red pepper flakes

SAUCE
*½ cup chicken stock (page 147) or fat-free, low-salt
   chicken broth*
2 ½ tablespoons low-sodium soy sauce
2 tablespoons Chinese rice wine or dry sherry
2 ½ tablespoons distilled white vinegar
¼ teaspoon sugar

1 tablespoon corn oil or peanut oil
2 small carrots, cut diagonally into ⅛-inch coins
1 large red bell pepper, seeded and cut into ½-inch squares
3 slender zucchini, cut into ¼-inch rounds
*1 tablespoon cornstarch dissolved in 2 tablespoons cold
   chicken stock or water*
Diagonally cut green and white scallion rings for garnish

Cut off squid tentacles and reserve. Cut off eye portion and discard. Run the blunt side of a knife along squid from base to head, and press out innards. Reach into cavity to pull out quill, and discard with innards. Peel off and discard any skin that clings to body. Cut the squid body crosswise into rings ¼ inch thick. Put into a colander with tentacles and flush well with cold water. You can do this ahead and set aside covered in refrigerator.

Combine the aromatics in a small dish, cover and set aside. Combine the sauce ingredients in a bowl, stirring to dissolve the sugar, and set aside.

To cook the squid, bring a medium-size saucepan of water to a boil. Using a Chinese mesh spoon or wire basket, lower squid into water and blanch just until white and firm, 6 seconds for body rings and 10 seconds for tentacles. Remove and plunge into a container of ice water to stop the cooking. Drain and set aside.

About 15 minutes before serving, heat a wok or large heavy skillet over high heat. Add the oil, turn heat to medium, then stir-fry the aromatics until fully fragrant, about 20 seconds. Add the carrots and toss for 1 minute, then add the bell pepper and toss for 2 minutes. Add the zucchini and toss to combine, about 1 minute.

Stir the sauce and add it to the pan. Bring sauce to a simmer. Cover the pan and cook until the vegetables are crisp tender, 1 to 2 minutes. Stir the cornstarch mixture, add it to the pan and stir until the sauce turns glossy, about 15 seconds.

Turn off the heat and fold in the drained squid. Serve immediately on heated plates, garnished with scallion rings.

*Yield: 2 main-course servings (serves 3 or 4 as part of a
multicourse meal).*
Per serving: 307 calories, 25 g protein, 28 g carbohydrates, 9 g fat (1 g saturated), 198 mg cholesterol, 705 mg sodium.

An East-Meets-West Sandwich
Ken Hom

This is a sandwich I created for the two-hundredth anniversary of Lord Sandwich's death, an event sponsored by the famous Parisian bread baker, Lionel Poilâne. The sandwich paired many of the flavors I've enjoyed with my friends and family from Hong Kong to Paris, and it's easy to make.

4 salmon fillets (4 ounces each)
¼ cup ginger juice squeezed from 5 ounces fresh ginger
  (page 149)
½ cup mirin (Japanese sweet rice wine)
Salt to taste
2 to 3 tablespoons Ken Hom's Peppercorn-Allspice Mixture
  (recipe follows)

East-West Persillade
3 tablespoons finely chopped fresh ginger
⅓ cup finely chopped scallions
Salt and freshly ground pepper to taste
3 tablespoons olive oil
¼ cup finely chopped fresh cilantro
¼ cup finely chopped fresh curly parsley
¼ cup finely chopped fresh Italian parsley
1 tablespoon finely chopped garlic

4 pieces fresh French bread
12 spinach leaves, well washed
16 to 20 dark opal basil leaves or regular basil leaves
2 large ripe tomatoes, thinly sliced

Rub the salmon fillets with the ginger juice and mirin. Add salt to the peppercorn-allspice mixture, mix together and sprinkle evenly on both sides of the salmon. Let the salmon marinate in a nonreactive dish at room temperature for at least 30 minutes.

Prepare the persillade mixture: In a small heatproof bowl, combine the ginger, scallions, salt and pepper. In a small skillet, heat the olive oil until it is quite hot but not smoking. Pour the hot oil over the ginger-scallion mixture. Scrape the mixture into a blender with the cilantro, both parsleys and garlic, and purée. Set aside.

Gently steam the salmon fillets over simmering water in a covered wok with a trivet or in a bamboo or metal steamer for 5 minutes, just until done. Or cover the fillets with plastic wrap and microwave at full power for 3 minutes. Let the salmon cool.

Preheat the oven to 350 degrees F and warm the bread for 5 minutes. Cut each piece in half lengthwise and scrape out the inside. Spread the persillade on the inside of the bread. Lay in the salmon, spinach, basil and tomato. Serve at once.

Yield: 4 servings.
Per serving: 430 calories, 28 g protein, 33 g carbohydrates, 19 g fat (2 g saturated), 63 mg cholesterol, 121 mg sodium.

Ken Hom's Peppercorn-Allspice Mixture
2 teaspoons Sichuan peppercorns, toasted (page 150)
2 teaspoons black peppercorns
2 teaspoons white peppercorns
2 teaspoons pink peppercorns
2 teaspoons green peppercorns
2 teaspoons whole allspice

Grind each ingredient, using a spice grinder or mortar and pestle, and mix together in a small bowl. It's a potent spice mixture, and since you'll probably grind more than you need, reserve the rest for another use. Store in a tightly sealed container at room temperature.

Yield: ¼ cup.

SARDINES WITH FENNEL, SWEET ONION, RAISINS AND SUN-DRIED TOMATO
Mary Etta Moose

Here is an appetizer and salad combination that might also serve as a light entrée. I'm suggesting tinned sardines, but fresh sardines, which come on the market around mid-March, are delicious in this dish. Before using, they should be gutted and grilled; or anointed with olive oil spray, salt and pepper, and baked. The bones provide calcium and a pleasant crunch.

2 tablespoons dry sherry
3 tablespoons (1 ounce) raisins
4 or 5 sun-dried tomatoes
2 tablespoons extra-virgin olive oil
1/2 teaspoon fennel seeds, toasted and ground (page 150)
8 sardines (from 2 water-packed tins, 3 3/4 ounces each)
1 sweet onion (such as Spanish red, Vidalia, Maui, Walla Walla or Bermuda), thinly sliced
1 bulb fennel with tops and leaves
Zest and juice of 1 lime
Salt and freshly ground pepper to taste

Place the sherry, raisins and tomatoes in a nonreactive saucepan and heat for 2 minutes to boiling. Remove from heat and soak the raisins and tomatoes in the sherry for at least 1/2 hour.

Gently bring the olive oil to a point of fragrance in a skillet over low heat, about 2 minutes, and add the ground fennel seeds. Set aside to infuse.

Drain the sardines, lay out on 4 serving plates and spoon the fennel-infused oil over them. Grind pepper over them and cover with onion slices.

Trim the root end of the fennel and shave off very fine slices of the bulb with a mandoline-style slicer or sharp knife. Mince and reserve the feathery leaves. Cover the onion layer with fennel slices and spoon the lime juice and zest evenly over the fennel. Salt and pepper lightly.

Strain the raisins and tomatoes over a bowl. Spoon the

liquid over the salad. Mince the tomatoes and sprinkle tomato pieces and raisins over the salad. Hold at room temperature for 15 minutes to an hour before serving for flavors to marry. Scatter a bit of the minced fennel leaves over all for garnish.

Yield: 4 servings.
Per serving: 215 calories, 12 g protein, 16 g carbohydrates, 9 g fat (2 g saturated), 34 mg cholesterol, 750 mg sodium.

GRILLED PRAWNS WITH PAPAYA SALSA
Paula LeDuc

This dish goes well with warm flour tortillas as wrappers for the prawns and salsa, and optional condiments such as arugula, sliced scallions and crème fraîche or yogurt. Guests can build their own combination. The dish is equally wonderful with grilled sea bass or salmon.

1 tablespoon olive oil
2 cloves garlic, finely chopped
1 tablespoon finely chopped fresh ginger
Salt and freshly ground pepper to taste
16 large prawns (about 1 pound), peeled and deveined

PAPAYA SALSA
1 ripe papaya, peeled, seeded and diced into 1/4-inch cubes
1/2 red bell pepper, seeded and finely chopped
1 large ripe tomato, peeled, seeded and diced
2 tablespoons finely chopped fresh chives
2 tablespoons finely chopped fresh cilantro
1 to 2 tablespoons fresh lime juice
1 jalapeño chili, seeded and finely chopped, or to taste
Salt and white pepper to taste

In a medium-size bowl, combine the olive oil, garlic, ginger, salt and pepper. Add the prawns, cover, refrigerate and marinate for at least 2 hours.

To prepare the salsa, combine the ingredients in another bowl and set aside for at least 1 hour to allow flavors to blend.

Preheat the grill. Grill the pawns over a fine grid just until they are pink, about 2 minutes on each side. You may also sauté the prawns in a hot skillet coated with olive oil. Cook over medium heat for 3 to 4 minutes. Serve the prawns topped with salsa.

Yield: 4 servings.
Per serving: 193 calories, 25 g protein, 12 g carbohydrates, 4.9 g fat (.8 g saturated), 221 mg cholesterol, 262 mg sodium.

TANDOORI-STYLE BARBECUED PRAWNS OVER MIXED GREENS
Irene Trias

This is a lighter version of an ancient Indian tandoori-barbecued prawn dish that I created at Appam restaurant, where I incorporate fresh California ingredients in my Indian recipes. Our customers love it as an appetizer or main course.

PRAWN MARINADE
1 cup low-fat plain yogurt
¼ cup fresh lemon juice
6 green cardamom seeds, crushed
2 tablespoons minced fresh ginger
1 tablespoon olive oil
1 tablespoon ground turmeric
2 teaspoons paprika
¼ teaspoon cayenne pepper (optional)
Salt to taste

1 ½ pounds prawns, peeled and deveined
¼ pound mixed baby salad greens
Juice of 1 lemon

In a large nonreactive bowl, mix together all the ingredients for the prawn marinade. In another nonreactive bowl, pour half the marinade over the prawns, completely coating them. Cover, refrigerate and marinate for about 1 hour.

Preheat the grill or broiler. Brush excess marinade from prawns. Grill the prawns on a fine grid until they turn pink, 1 to 2 minutes on each side, or place them on a broiler rack and broil for 1 to 2 minutes on each side. Brush remaining marinade over prawns as they finish cooking.

Place the greens in a salad bowl, squeeze lemon juice over them and toss. Place the prawns on the greens and serve promptly.

Yield: 4 servings.
Per serving: 266 calories, 39 g protein, 11 g carbohydrates, 6 g fat (1 g saturated), 335 mg cholesterol, 432 mg sodium.

THAI-STYLE PRAWN CAKES
Kirk Webber

I think you'll love these Thai-style prawn cakes because they're so simple to prepare and are healthy for you. At Cafe Kati, I always veer toward foods that are packed with flavor, such as this dish with its basic Asian ingredients. It proves that you don't need a whole lot of calories for food to taste good. The Asian ingredients, including the kaffir lime leaves (which may be omitted) and lemongrass, are usually stocked by Thai grocers, but are sometimes sold at other Asian markets and better supermarkets. If you wish, serve the prawn cakes with a mixed green salad.

FISH-SAUCE VINAIGRETTE
1/4 cup Asian fish sauce
1/4 cup rice vinegar
1 tablespoon plus 1 teaspoon light corn syrup
1 teaspoon minced garlic
2 tablespoons finely sliced scallions
1/2 teaspoon Asian chili paste, or to taste

1 pound prawns, peeled and deveined
2 tablespoons Asian fish sauce
1 teaspoon Asian chili paste, or to taste
1 small stalk lemongrass, trimmed of tough tops and outer
  layers and finely minced, or
1 teaspoon lemongrass powder
8 kaffir lime leaves (optional), soaked if dried (page 150)
  and finely minced
Salt to taste
1/3 cup finely sliced fresh mint leaves
Parchment paper

To prepare the vinaigrette, combine the ingredients in a small bowl. Whisk until well mixed and set aside.

In a food processor, process prawns in short bursts, leaving them still chunky, or chop them with a chef's knife. Add the fish sauce, chili paste, lemongrass, kaffir lime leaves, if using, and salt. Process again, using short bursts, until mixed. Stir in the mint leaves.

Preheat the oven to 425 degrees F. Shape the mixture into 1-inch round cakes. Place on a baking sheet lined with parchment paper and bake in oven for 5 minutes, just until cooked through. Serve 3 cakes per person with fish sauce vinaigrette on the side.

Yield: 6 servings.
Per serving: 111 calories, 19 g protein, 5 g carbohydrates, 1 g fat (.2 g saturated), 158 mg cholesterol, 330 mg sodium.

MANDARIN QUAIL WITH GINGER JUICE AND CINNAMON OIL
Ercolino Crugnale

This quail recipe makes a sensational appetizer, especially if the quail are grilled over a charcoal fire. Since the cinnamon oil is an infusion that requires three days to prepare, you may not want to bother, and, if you wish, you can serve the dish without it. But you'll be amazed at the unique flavor exuded from the combination with the quail. I recommend a Rhône-style red wine or Zinfandel with the dish.

CINNAMON OIL
1/4 cup ground cinnamon
1/4 cup warm water
Salt to taste
3 tablespoons canola oil

QUAIL MARINADE
1 tablespoon Asian sesame oil
3 tablespoons honey
3 tablespoons low-sodium soy sauce
2 tablespoons molasses
1/3 cup finely minced scallions

4 quail, cleaned and deboned
Salt and freshly ground pepper to taste
1 tablespoon canola oil or canola oil spray
1/2 cup shredded napa cabbage
3 tablespoons diced and seeded yellow bell pepper
3 tablespoons diced and seeded red bell pepper
3 tablespoons diagonally sliced scallions
1 small carrot, cut into julienne strips
3 tablespoons snipped fresh chives (1/2 inch long)
2 tablespoons rice vinegar
1 tablespoon fresh ginger juice (page 149)
1 tablespoon toasted sesame seeds (page 150)

To prepare the cinnamon oil, combine the cinnamon, water and salt in a bowl. Whisk together well, then stir in the canola oil. Transfer to a covered container, preferably glass, and let sit for 3 days at room temperature. After 3 days, spoon the oil off the top, discarding the sediment, or strain through a fine sieve. Store the cinnamon oil in an airtight container in the refrigerator.

Combine the marinade ingredients in a shallow nonreactive bowl, add the quail, spooning the marinade over them. Marinate for no more than 1 hour. Remove quail from the marinade and season lightly with salt and pepper.

Preheat the grill or heat a large skillet coated or sprayed with canola oil over medium heat. Grill the quail, or sauté them, until nicely browned, about 4 to 5 minutes on each side. If you like the quail well done, cook a minute longer.

Meanwhile, combine the cabbage, red and yellow peppers, scallions, carrot and chives in a nonreactive bowl. Toss with the rice vinegar and season with salt and pepper.

To serve, place the salad at the top of the plate, with the quail just below the salad. Drizzle the cinnamon oil and ginger juice around the quail. Sprinkle with sesame seeds.

Yield: 4 servings.
Per serving: 309 calories, 22 g protein, 29 g carbohydrates, 12 g fat (2 g saturated), 64 mg cholesterol, 634 mg sodium.

TWOFOLD PROSPERITY CLAMS
Andy Wai

This is a traditional Chinese New Year's dish, but my family enjoys it the year round because it's healthy and tasty, and a nice diversion from the usual fish or chicken. Besides, these clams are supposed to bring double prosperity to those who feast on them.

1 pound clams in the shell (preferably littleneck)
2 tablespoons rock salt

1 1/2 tablespoons Chinese fermented black beans
1 large clove garlic, crushed
1 tablespoon plus 1 teaspoon peanut oil
1 tablespoon cornstarch
1/2 cup cold chicken stock (page 147) or canned fat-free, low-salt chicken broth
1/2 teaspoon sugar
1/4 teaspoon Asian sesame oil
2 teaspoons dry sherry
1 hot green chili (such as jalapeño or serrano), seeded and diced
1/2 red bell pepper, seeded and diced
1 scallion, chopped
Salt and freshly ground pepper to taste
2 cups cooked white rice

Place the clams and rock salt in a large bowl of cold water to cover for 30 minutes. Drain and rinse clams well. Set aside.

Place the black beans, garlic and 1 teaspoon peanut oil in a medium bowl and, with the back of a spoon, mash them into a smooth paste. Set aside.

In a small bowl, stir together the cornstarch and chicken stock. Set aside.

In a large skillet or wok, heat 1 tablespoon peanut oil over high heat until oil is bubbly. Reduce heat to medium and place the clams in the skillet. Add the sugar, sesame oil, sherry, chili pepper, red bell pepper and scallion, and stir well. Cook covered for 3 to 5 minutes, until clams are just open. (It's important not to overcook clams.) Discard any clams that do not open.

Uncover the skillet, add the black bean mixture and stir well. Then add the cornstarch mixture, season with salt and pepper, and heat through, while stirring, for about 1/2 minute.

Serve promptly over warm rice.

Yield: 2 servings as a light entrée
(more if part of a multi-course meal).
Per serving: 461 calories, 19 g protein, 66 g carbohydrates, 11 g fat (1 g saturated), 28 mg cholesterol, 248 mg sodium.

TURKEY CHILI WITH TOMATILLOS
Kelly Mills

I thought of doing a turkey chili to accommodate my restaurant customers who want a luncheon dish that's hearty, inexpensive and fairly low in calories. Essentially, it's a traditional chili with turkey in place of beef, and it's the kind of dish that's not just good and healthy, but it sticks to the bones.

2 teaspoons olive oil
2 pounds coarsely ground turkey meat
Salt and freshly ground pepper to taste
1 large yellow onion, cut into ¹/₂-inch dice
1 red bell pepper, seeded and cut into ¹/₂-inch dice
1 green bell pepper, seeded and cut into ¹/₂-inch dice
1 tablespoon minced garlic
1 teaspoon cumin seeds
2 tablespoons chili powder
1 tablespoon dried oregano
2 tablespoons tomato paste
1 jar (16 ounces) mild green chili salsa
2 cups cooked black beans
Cayenne pepper to taste
1 pound tomatillos, husked, rinsed in hot water and cut into
*   1-inch dice*
¹/₃ cup chopped fresh cilantro
Nonfat sour cream for garnish

Heat the olive oil in a large nonstick skillet over medium heat. Add the turkey meat, season with salt and pepper, and sauté until lightly browned, about 10 minutes. Drain off excess fat from pan. Add the onion, red and green pepper, garlic, cumin seeds, chili powder and oregano, and sauté until onion is tender, about 5 minutes. Add the tomato paste and cook 2 more minutes, stirring well. Add the salsa and cooked black beans, season with salt and pepper, and cook until the meat is tender, about 5 more minutes. Check the seasoning, and, if needed, add cayenne.

Serve the chili in bowls topped with tomatillo and chopped cilantro. Garnish with a dollop of sour cream.

Yield: 8 servings.
297 calories, 37 g protein, 18 g carbohydrates, 8 g fat (2 g saturated), 85 mg cholesterol, 334 mg sodium.

FLAT BREAD TOSTADA WITH BLACK BEANS, POACHED EGG AND TOMATILLO SALSA
Cindy Pawlcyn

Here's a dish that evolved from a flat bread recipe that I found in Carlo Middione's cookbook, *The Food of Southern Italy*. I use the parchment-thin cracker bread in a non-Italian way—for a tostada with a topping of black beans, poached egg and tomatillo salsa. The beans are made in a two-step process with the addition of soy sauce and cardamom. It's a terrific trick that I learned from Gordon Drysdale, the chef at Bix. If you're not eating eggs, try the tostada with roasted peppers, sliced tomatoes from the garden and the salsa. The flat bread is baked on a baking stone, also called a pizza stone. It's made of heat-resistant ceramic and sold in most cookware stores. if you don't have time to make the flat bread, you can substitute toasted tortillas.

FLAT BREAD
¹/₂ cup semolina flour
1 cup all-purpose flour, plus flour for dusting work surface
¹/₄ teaspoon salt
¹/₂ to ³/₄ cup warm water

TOMATILLO SALSA

2 pounds tomatillos, husked and rinsed in hot water
1/2 cup diced red onion
2 tablespoons minced scallion (white part only)
1/4 cup chopped fresh cilantro
1 1/2 jalapeño chilies, seeded and minced
Salt and freshly ground pepper to taste

BLACK BEANS

2 cups dried black beans (13 ounces)
2 small yellow onions, diced
2 teaspoons olive oil
2 cloves garlic, minced
2 teaspoons ground cardamom
2 teaspoons ground cumin
1/2 teaspoon chili powder
1/2 teaspoon freshly ground pepper
3 tablespoons low-sodium soy sauce
1/2 large red bell pepper, seeded and diced
3 1/2 cups chicken stock (page 147) or vegetable stock
   (page 148) or water
6 fresh basil leaves, cut into thin strips
1 teaspoon Cindy Pawlcyn's Chili Paste (recipe follows)
Juice of 1 lime
Salt to taste

6 eggs
3 cups water
1 teaspoon sea salt
1 teaspoon rice vinegar or other mild vinegar
Nonfat plain yogurt and fresh cilantro sprigs for garnish

To prepare the flat bread, combine both flours and salt in a large bowl, gradually add the water and mix until you have a soft dough. Let rest for 20 minutes.

Preheat the oven with a baking stone to 450 degrees F. Divide the dough into 6 equal-size pieces. On a floured surface, roll out the pieces very thin, to about 1/16-inch thickness. Bake on baking stone for 2 to 2 1/2 minutes per side, turning back and forth until lightly golden and crisp. The flat breads may be stored in a tightly sealed tin or container. They can be rewarmed in a hot oven.

To prepare the tomatillo salsa, preheat the grill or broiler. Place the tomatillos on grill or under broiler and roast until skins are charred and blistered, about 5 minutes. Place tomatillos in blender or food processor and purée. Strain through a medium sieve into a bowl and mix in all other salsa ingredients. Season with salt and pepper. (Makes about 3 cups.) Cover and set aside in the refrigerator.

To prepare the black beans, wash them and check for stones. In a medium-size, heavy-bottomed saucepan, cook half the diced onions in 1 teaspoon olive oil over medium heat until soft and lightly browned, about 5 minutes. Add the garlic, 1 teaspoon of the cardamom, 1 teaspoon of the cumin, the chili powder and the pepper. Cook 1 minute. Add the beans, soy sauce and enough water to cover the beans, and bring to a boil. Reduce heat and cook the beans at a simmer until they are tender. The cooking time will depend on the freshness of the beans. They can take anywhere from 1/2 hour to 1 1/2 hours. When done, drain the beans and spread them on a baking sheet to cool. The beans may be made a day ahead up to this point.

To finish the beans, use a large, nonstick skillet or heavy-bottomed saucepan. Sauté the diced bell pepper and remaining diced onion in 1 teaspoon olive oil over medium heat until soft, about 5 minutes. Add the cooked beans, stock or water, 1 teaspoon cumin, 1 teaspoon cardamom, the fresh basil and chili paste. Cook until hot and saucy, about 15 minutes. Just before serving, add the lime juice and season with salt and, if needed, more pepper.

When ready to serve, poach the eggs. In a wide saucepan, bring water, salt and vinegar to a boil. Lower heat and slide an egg into the simmering liquid and poach to your desired degree of doneness, basting occasionally, about 5 to 6 minutes. Lift out with a slotted spoon and drain on paper towels. To serve, place rewarmed flat bread on a plate, top with 1/2 cup beans, a poached egg and some tomatillo sauce. Garnish with a drizzle of yogurt and a cilantro sprig.

Yield: 6 servings.
Per serving: 331 calories, 16 g protein, 48 g carbohydrates,
8 g fat (2 g saturated), 215 mg cholesterol, 669 mg sodium.

CINDY PAWLCYN'S CHILI PASTE
2 ancho or cascabel chilies
2 pasilla chilies
2 guajillo chilies

    To make this chili paste, you can vary the combination of dried chilies, depending on your preference and the availability in your area.

    Preheat the oven to 350 degrees F. Stem and seed the chilies. Place them on a baking sheet and toast in the oven until they are fragrant, 5 to 8 minutes. Place the chilies in a medium-size bowl, add hot water to cover and soak until soft. Drain off all but ¹/₂ cup of water. Transfer the chilies and reserved water to a blender and purée until smooth, then rub through a sieve. Set aside covered in refrigerator. Since you'll be making more chili paste than you need, save the rest for other uses.

Yield: 1 ¹/₄ cup.

TOFU-VEGETABLE SCRAMBLE
Margaret Fox

Customers at Cafe Beaujolais, my restaurant in Mendocino, wanted an egg-free breakfast dish. We concocted this, and it has become one of our most popular items. It's hearty and healthy and can include as many of the suggested vegetables as you wish.

1 cup crumbled firm tofu
1 ¹/₂ teaspoons cumin seeds, toasted and ground (page 150)
1 teaspoon (or more to taste) chili paste or spicy salsa

¹/₂ teaspoon salt
Pinch of cayenne pepper
3 cups diced potatoes (about 1 pound)
6 cloves garlic, roasted and mashed (page 149)
3 cups assorted vegetables, such as diced roasted red bell
   pepper (page 150), diced green bell pepper, sliced scallion,
   diced zucchini, diced carrot, broccoli florets and/or
   corn kernels
2 tablespoons canola oil or olive oil
¹/₄ cup diced celery
Salt and freshly ground pepper to taste
2 to 4 whole wheat tortillas
¹/₄ cup cooked black beans
Chopped fresh cilantro for garnish

    In a medium-size bowl, combine the tofu, cumin, chili paste or salsa, salt and cayenne. Set aside.

    Cook the diced potatoes in a saucepan of lightly salted simmering water over medium heat, just until tender, about 10 minutes. Drain and set aside.

    In a medium-size bowl, combine the garlic and vegetable assortment. If using carrot, blanch in boiling salted water for 5 minutes before combining. If using broccoli florets, blanch in boiling salted water for 1 minute. Set aside.

    In a 12-inch skillet, heat oil over medium heat and sauté potatoes until crisp and brown, about 10 minutes. Add celery and sauté briefly, then add the tofu mixture and vegetable mixture. Season with salt and pepper. Cook just until vegetables are done, about 5 minutes. Serve with warmed whole wheat tortillas and a dollop of black beans. Garnish generously with chopped cilantro.

Yield: 4 servings.
Per serving: 348 calories, 13 g protein, 54 g carbohydrates,
11 g fat (1 g saturated), 0 mg cholesterol, 334 mg sodium.

Stir-Fried Garlic Chicken with Cilantro
Anne and David Gingrass

A spicy, zesty, Asian-influenced dish with lots of flavor and very little fat, this stir-fry was one of our more popular items at Postrio. Though usually served as an appetizer, it makes an excellent lunch entrée.

2 pounds coarsely ground boneless and skinless chicken
  (leg meat is ideal)
1 teaspoon chili flakes, or more to your taste
4 tablespoons finely chopped garlic
4 tablespoons finely chopped fresh ginger
3 tablespoons extra-virgin olive oil
1/4 cup red wine vinegar
1/4 cup low-sodium soy sauce
1/2 cup demi-glace (page 147) or canned beef broth
4 scallions, thinly sliced
Leaves from 2 bunches fresh cilantro
1/4 cup sherry vinegar
1 teaspoon Dijon mustard
Salt and freshly ground pepper to taste
8 cups loosely packed julienned spinach leaves
24 outer leaves radicchio
Fresh cilantro sprigs for garnish

In a large bowl, combine the ground chicken with the chili flakes and 2 tablespoons each of the garlic and ginger. Mix gently until flavorings are evenly distributed.

To prepare the stir-fried chicken, heat a wok or large skillet until very hot. Add 1 tablespoon of the olive oil, then the chicken mixture. Stir-fry slowly over medium heat, allowing the meat to brown lightly. Add the remaining 2 tablespoons each garlic and ginger and stir-fry quickly over high heat until fragrant, then add the red wine vinegar, soy sauce and demi-glace. With the pan still on high heat, let the liquid reduce until it begins to coat the meat. Remove the pan from the heat and add the scallions and cilantro; then toss to mix thoroughly.

Make a vinaigrette for the spinach in a large salad bowl by whisking together 2 tablespoons olive oil with the sherry vinegar, mustard, salt and pepper. Toss the spinach with the vinaigrette to coat it lightly. Place 3 radicchio leaves on each plate, then fill the leaves with the spinach salad. Spoon a small amount of the stir-fried chicken over the spinach and garnish with cilantro sprigs.

Yield: 8 servings.
Per serving: 206 calories, 29 g protein, 6 g carbohydrates, 6 g fat (1 g saturated), 65 mg cholesterol, 597 mg sodium.

salads

SPRING VEGETABLE SALAD
Gérald Hirigoyen

COOL SUMMER VEGETABLE SALAD
Carol Field

SHAVED FENNEL SALAD WITH BLOOD ORANGE VINAIGRETTE
AND CHEESE CROUTON
Lance Dean Velasquez

BUTTER LETTUCE AND SPINACH SALAD WITH PINE NUTS
AND ROASTED GARLIC-HONEY DRESSING
Donna Katzl

PLUM, BASIL AND RED ONION SALAD
Lenore Nolan-Ryan

COMPOSED VEGETABLE SALAD WITH TONNATO SAUCE
Lenore Nolan-Ryan

SUMMER BEAN AND CORN SALAD
Bradley Ogden

GREEN BEAN SALAD WITH FIRE WALNUTS
Paul Kavouksorian

ASPARAGUS WITH RED ONION VINAIGRETTE
Gary Danko

CRAB AND MANGO SALAD
Patricia Unterman

✤

Spring Vegetable Salad
Gérald Hirigoyen

This simple salad is made of a colorful assortment of spring vegetables that are cooked separately so the flavors remain clean and distinct. The lemon vinaigrette is tangy and vibrant, yet does not distract from the fresh, crisp vegetables.

4 medium-size artichoke hearts, sliced
8 baby golden beets (10 ounces)
8 baby carrots (10 ounces)
1 cup green unshelled peas (4 ounces)
1 cup fava beans (about 6 ounces with pods)
12 medium-size asparagus (10 ounces)
12 snow peas (4 ounces)
Juice of 2 lemons
2 tablespoons extra-virgin olive oil
Salt and freshly ground pepper to taste
Leaves from 1 sprig fresh chervil
5 fresh basil leaves, finely chopped
1/4 cup finely chopped fresh chives

Blanch all the vegetables separately in a saucepan of lightly salted boiling water over medium heat, just until tender. Cook the artichokes for 25 to 30 minutes, the beets for 15 minutes, the carrots for 5 to 7 minutes, the peas, fava beans and asparagus for 3 to 5 minutes, and the snow peas for 2 to 3 minutes.

As soon as each vegetable is finished cooking, plunge into a bowl of ice water to halt the cooking process. Remove immediately and drain in a colander.

Prepare a vinaigrette in a small bowl by whisking together the lemon juice, olive oil, salt and pepper. Combine the blanched vegetables, chervil, basil, chives and vinaigrette in a serving bowl, and toss gently. *Et voilà!* The salad is ready to serve.

Yield: 4 servings.
Per serving: 247 calories, 10 g protein, 38 g carbohydrates, 7 g fat (1 g saturated), 0 mg cholesterol, 549 mg sodium.

Cool Summer Vegetable Salad
Carol Field

I love the versatility of this summery vegetable mixture. It can be spooned onto grilled slices of country bread, it can double as a delicious antipasto course or it can be tossed into cooled curls of pasta to become a summer salad.

1 small red onion, diced
1/2 cucumber, peeled, seeded and diced
2 full-flavored ripe tomatoes
1 teaspoon sea salt
1/8 teaspoon dried oregano
1/4 cup finely chopped fresh Italian parsley
1/4 cup finely shredded fresh basil
Scant 1/8 teaspoon red pepper flakes
1 tablespoon extra-virgin olive oil
Salt and freshly ground pepper to taste

Set the diced onion and cucumber in a bowl. Bring a pot of water to the boil, drop in the tomatoes for a minute, remove, and slide off the skins. Seed and dice the tomatoes and add to the bowl. Sprinkle with the salt and leave for 2 hours.

Drain any liquid from the vegetables and stir in the oregano, parsley, basil and red pepper flakes. Toss with the olive oil and season with salt and pepper. Serve as an appetizer or as an antipasto salad.

Yield: 4 servings.
Per serving: 57 calories, 1 g protein, 6 g carbohydrates, 3 g fat (.5 g saturated), 0 mg cholesterol, 542 mg sodium.

SHAVED FENNEL SALAD WITH BLOOD ORANGE VINAIGRETTE AND CHEESE CROUTON
Lance Dean Velasquez

Here's an elegant, colorful, hearty salad that's as appealing for its crisp, bracing texture as for its lively combination of flavors. Serve it for lunch as an accompaniment to cold poached salmon or by itself as a first course for dinner.

2 small bulbs young fennel
3 blood oranges

BLOOD ORANGE VINAIGRETTE
1 cup fresh blood orange juice (squeezed from
  approximately 4 oranges)
½ teaspoon coriander seeds, toasted and crushed (page 150)
¼ teaspoon fennel seeds, toasted and crushed (page 150)
1 tablespoon champagne vinegar
2 tablespoons olive oil or canola oil
Salt and freshly ground pepper to taste

6 slices sourdough French baguette
4 ounces reduced-fat creamy cheese (such as Havarti
  or Jarlsberg)
Leaves from 2 heads of red leaf lettuce (such as Lollo Rosa)
  and/or 2 to 3 cups mixed field greens

Trim and discard the bruised outer leaves and stems from the fennel. Soak the trimmed fennel bulbs in a large bowl of cold water for 3 to 4 minutes. Remove and shake off excess water in a salad spinner or pat dry with a clean dish towel. Refrigerate the fennel in a bowl covered with a damp towel.

Halve the 3 blood oranges and remove segments with a grapefruit knife, working over a bowl to catch the fruit and juice. Squeeze shells for remaining juice and add to the cup of orange juice.

To prepare the vinaigrette, pour the orange juice into a nonreactive saucepan and add the crushed coriander and fennel seeds. Cook over medium heat until reduced by half. Strain through a fine strainer into a large bowl and set aside to cool.

When cool, add vinegar and oil to orange juice and whisk well. Season with salt and pepper. Set aside.

Shave the fennel very thin with a mandoline-style slicer or sharp knife and toss the shavings with the vinaigrette.

Preheat the broiler. Top each slice of bread with a slice of cheese. Place bread slices on a baking sheet and toast under the broiler until the cheese turns golden.

Toss the greens with the fennel, divide among 6 chilled plates and accent with the orange sections. Top each salad with a warm cheese crouton.

Yield: 6 servings.
Per serving: 215 calories, 8 g protein, 27 g carbohydrates, 8 g fat (2 g saturated), 7 mg cholesterol, 320 mg sodium.

BUTTER LETTUCE AND SPINACH SALAD
WITH PINE NUTS AND
ROASTED GARLIC-HONEY DRESSING
Donna Katzl

I'm proud of this salad, which I devised for a cooking class when I wanted something light to go with a lamb dish. It worked out well, and I've used it since in my menus at the Cafe for All Seasons because the roasted garlic dressing is so tasty and the fat content is so low. The salad can also be made with butter lettuce and no spinach, or with spinach and no butter lettuce.

Leaves from 1 large head butter lettuce, torn into
*   bite-size pieces*
2 cups baby spinach leaves (4 ounces)
¼ cup thinly sliced scallions
1 head garlic, roasted (page 149)
2 tablespoons Dijon mustard
¼ cup cider vinegar
1 tablespoon honey
2 tablespoons water
Salt and freshly ground pepper to taste
¼ cup lightly toasted pine nuts (page 150)

Combine the lettuce, spinach leaves and scallions in a salad bowl, cover with a damp cloth and set aside to chill in the refrigerator.

Squeeze the pulp from the skins of the roasted head of garlic into a small bowl, and mash. Add the mustard, vinegar, honey, water, and salt and pepper, and whisk together. Let the dressing sit at room temperature for at least 2 hours to blend the flavors. When ready to serve, pour the dressing on the salad, sprinkle on pine nuts and toss gently.

Yield: 6 servings.
Per serving: 81 calories, 3 g protein, 8 g carbohydrates, 5 g fat (.7 g saturated), 0 mg cholesterol, 176 mg sodium.

PLUM, BASIL AND RED ONION SALAD
Lenore Nolan-Ryan

This salad is wonderful as a light lunch eaten with low-fat ricotta cheese and a good dark bread. It works well, too, served on a bed of mixed greens or as an accompaniment to an entrée of grilled chicken or pork.

10 ripe plums (preferably Satsuma)
½ medium-size red onion
⅓ cup honey
½ cup fresh lemon juice
24 small basil leaves
Salt and freshly ground pepper to taste

Pit the plums and cut them into eighths. Thinly slice the red onion lengthwise into quarter moons. In a large bowl, mix together the honey and lemon juice. Gently toss the plums, onion slices and basil leaves with the honey-lemon mixture. Season with salt and pepper.

Yield: 4 servings.
Per serving: 141 calories, 1 g protein, 36 g carbohydrates, .5 g fat (.05 saturated), 0 mg cholesterol, 135 mg sodium.

COMPOSED VEGETABLE SALAD
WITH TONNATO SAUCE
Lenore Nolan-Ryan

To serve with a main course, this salad and sauce go well with grilled, oven-roasted or poached fish, chicken or veal, as in the classic *vitello tonnato* (veal with tuna sauce). The salad is also a great addition to any buffet.

TONNATO SAUCE
2 medium-size yellow onions, sliced
4 cloves garlic, sliced
3 anchovy fillets
Bouquet garni of 2 sprigs fresh thyme, 3 black peppercorns
*   and ¹/₂ sliced lemon, tied in cheesecloth*
1 cup white wine
1 can (6 ¹/₈ ounces) water-packed white tuna, drained
1 cup nonfat sour cream
1 cup nonfat mayonnaise
2 tablespoons fresh lemon juice
Salt and freshly ground pepper to taste

1 pound small red potatoes (cut in half, if you wish)
1 pound baby carrots
¹/₂ pound green beans
1 pound asparagus
2 cups (8 ounces) broccoli florets
4 ounces snow peas
1 red, 1 green and 1 yellow bell pepper, seeded and cut
*   into julienne strips*
1 cup cherry tomatoes (10 ounces)
Hearts from 2 heads romaine lettuce
Lemon wedges and fresh thyme sprigs for garnish

In a small, nonreactive saucepan, simmer the sliced onion, garlic, anchovies, bouquet garni and white wine over low heat until the wine has evaporated, about 6 minutes. Remove the bouquet garni.

Transfer contents of the pan to a food processor or blender, add the tuna and purée. Blend in the sour cream, mayonnaise, lemon juice, and salt and pepper. Process until smooth. Remove sauce to a container, cover and refrigerate until ready to use.

In a medium-size saucepan, blanch the vegetables separately (except the bell peppers and cherry tomatoes, which are served raw) until crisp tender in lightly salted boiling water. Cook the potatoes for 10 to 12 minutes, the carrots and green beans for 3 to 4 minutes, the asparagus and broccoli for 1 to 2 minutes and the snow peas for 30 seconds. As soon as each vegetable is cooked, plunge into a bowl of ice water for 1 minute to stop the cooking process, and drain in a colander.

Arrange the blanched vegetables with bell peppers, cherry tomatoes and romaine hearts on individual plates or on a large platter. Garnish with lemon wedges and thyme sprigs. Pass the tonnato sauce in a bowl.

Yield: 8 servings.
Per serving: 335 calories, 18 g protein, 63 g carbohydrates, 2 g fat (.4 g saturated), 7 mg cholesterol, 567 mg sodium.

Summer Bean and Corn Salad
Bradley Ogden

Remember the abundance of the summer market with its colorful array of fresh vegetables, like the tender green beans, sweet corn and ripe tomatoes called for in this salad? It's a perfect summer salad, fine by itself or with grilled chicken or fish. It's simple and quick to make, and flavorful enough to prepare without oil, which should appeal to those on diets. If you like, mix in some freshly cooked shell beans, fava beans or sweet peas.

1 pound Kentucky Wonder beans, or other fresh variety,
  stem end trimmed
½ cup fresh corn kernels (cut from 1 ear of corn)
Kosher salt and freshly ground pepper to taste
2 medium-size ripe tomatoes, peeled, seeded and diced
1 small cucumber, peeled, seeded and diced
½ cup finely diced red onion
½ teaspoon minced garlic
¼ cup chopped fresh basil
3 tablespoons chopped fresh chives
2 tablespoons white wine vinegar

In a medium-size saucepan, blanch the beans in boiling salted water just until tender, 2 to 4 minutes. Drain immediately and plunge into a bowl of ice water. Drain and place in a large bowl. Blanch the corn in boiling salted water for 1 minute, drain and plunge into ice water. Drain and combine with the beans. Season lightly with salt and pepper.

Add the rest of the ingredients to the bowl with beans and corn. Mix well. Adjust the seasoning. Arrange the salad on serving plates.

Yield: 4 servings.
Per serving: 90 calories, 4 g protein, 20 g carbohydrates, .8 g fat (.1 g saturated), 0 mg cholesterol, 285 mg sodium.

Green Bean Salad with Fire Walnuts
Paul Kavouksorian

The idea of an Asian-flavored green bean salad with very spicy toasted walnuts inspired this dish. It intrigues and even perplexes people since they can't quite figure out the secret of the fiery walnuts. But it could not be simpler or more forthright, and the dish is so quick and easy to make, it's a breeze.

½ cup walnut halves and pieces
Vegetable oil spray
½ teaspoon cayenne pepper
12 ounces slender green beans, cut into 3-inch pieces
2 tablespoons low-sodium soy sauce
1 tablespoon red wine vinegar
2 tablespoons canola oil or safflower oil
Salt to taste

Place the walnuts in a skillet, lightly coat with vegetable oil spray, sprinkle on the cayenne pepper and toss. Toast the walnuts over medium-low heat until fragrant and nicely browned, 4 to 5 minutes. Set aside.

In a medium-sized saucepan of boiling salted water, blanch the green beans over medium heat just until crisp tender, 2 to 4 minutes. Plunge the beans into a bowl of ice water to stop the cooking process. Drain and set aside.

Prepare a vinaigrette by combining the soy sauce, vinegar and oil in a medium-size bowl. Whisk until emulsified. Add salt, if needed. Toss the green beans with the vinaigrette and add the walnuts. Serve as an appetizer salad or as an accompaniment to an entrée.

Yield: 4 servings.
Per serving: 172 calories, 3 g protein, 9 g carbohydrates, 14 g fat (1 g saturated), 0 mg cholesterol, 420 mg sodium.

Asparagus with Red Onion Vinaigrette
Gary Danko

This recipe makes me think of spring when asparagus first appears in the markets and is so good to eat. You'll find this a very refreshing appetizer or salad. It has a mustard vinaigrette that acquires texture with the addition of capers and red onion, and is a nice contrast for the delicate asparagus.

2 pounds pencil-thin or medium asparagus
1 tablespoon tarragon vinegar
¼ teaspoon kosher salt
¼ teaspoon freshly ground pepper
1 tablespoon Dijon mustard
3 tablespoons extra-virgin olive oil
¼ cup finely chopped red onion
1 clove garlic, finely minced
2 tablespoons drained capers
2 tablespoons minced fresh tarragon or dill
1 tablespoon boiling water
2 red bell peppers, roasted, seeded and cut into ¼-inch
  strips (page 150)
6 tablespoons freshly grated or shaved Parmesan cheese
  (preferably Parmigiano Reggiano)
12 black oil-cured olives

Blanch the asparagus in a large pot of boiling salted water over medium heat just until tender, 1 to 2 minutes. Remove asparagus and plunge into a bowl of ice water for 1 minute. Drain and set aside.

In a small bowl, combine the vinegar, salt, pepper and mustard, and whisk in the olive oil, onion, garlic, capers and tarragon or dill. Whisk in the boiling water.

Arrange the asparagus on 6 plates, lattice the pepper strips at the base of the asparagus, drizzle the dressing over the asparagus and sprinkle Parmesan over the top. Garnish with olives and serve as a salad or appetizer.

Yield: 6 servings.
Per serving: 147 calories, 8 g protein, 9 g carbohydrates, 10 g fat (2 saturated), 4 mg cholesterol, 321 mg sodium.

Crab and Mango Salad
Patricia Unterman

We have done this simple crab salad at the Hayes Street Grill in many different variations. It is one of the most satisfying salads I know of that doesn't use any oil in the dressing. Of course, the ripeness and firm texture of the mangoes and the freshness and sweetness of the crabmeat are what carry the salad, so the search for ingredients in this case is more important than the preparation. Serve the salad with fresh sourdough bread.

8 ounces fresh cooked crabmeat
2 medium-size ripe mangoes, peeled and cut into
  ½-inch dice
Juice of 3 to 4 limes
1 small, hot, red chili, seeded and finely chopped
⅓ cup fresh cilantro leaves or thinly sliced fresh
  mint leaves, or both
Salt and freshly ground pepper to taste

In a large bowl, combine the crabmeat and mangoes and toss with the other ingredients. Season with salt and pepper, if needed.

Yield: 4 servings.
Per serving: 129 calories, 11 g protein, 19 g carbohydrates, 1.2 g fat (.2 g saturated), 37 mg cholesterol, 428 mg sodium.

pasta, rice and grains

WHOLE WHEAT PASTA WITH TOMATOES, OLIVES AND BASIL
Patrizio Sacchetto and Mark Herand

PASTA TUTTO FUNGHI
Gino Laghi

RAGOÛT OF SPICED WHITE VEGETABLES WITH PRUNE WONTONS
Mary Etta Moose

PENNE RIGATE PASTA WITH BABY ARTICHOKES AND SPINACH
Donna Katzl

DUNGENESS CRAB RAVIOLI WITH ASPARAGUS AND ANISE BROTH
Tom Switzer

LINGUINE WITH CHICKEN, SPINACH AND MUSTARD-DILL SAUCE
Charles Saunders

OXTAIL AND POTATO RAVIOLI IN VEGETABLE BROTH
Lance Dean Velasquez

SPICY TOFU WITH LINGUINE
Andy Wai

RISOTTO WITH WILD MUSHROOMS AND BABY ARTICHOKES
Walter Zolezzi

UDON SUKI
Maggie Waldron

POLENTA SOUFFLÉ AND GRILLED PORCINI MUSHROOMS
Robert Helstrom

VEGETABLE CURRY WITH APPLE COUSCOUS
Christopher L. Majer

Whole Wheat Pasta with Tomatoes, Olives and Basil
Patrizio Sacchetto and Mark Herand

The vibrant, harmonious flavors of this Piedmontese dish are uniquely Italian, but the ingredients could not be simpler or more readily available. The whole wheat pasta, with neither the wheat germ nor bran removed, is full of nutty flavor and could not be healthier for you.

12 ounces dried whole wheat fettuccine or spaghetti
1 tablespoon olive oil
2 cloves garlic, thinly sliced
4 Roma (plum) tomatoes, peeled, seeded and diced
1/2 cup kalamata olives, pitted and chopped
Leaves from 1 bunch fresh basil, thinly sliced
1/3 cup chicken stock (page 147) or canned fat-free,
*   low-salt chicken broth*
Salt and freshly ground pepper to taste
3/4 cup freshly grated Parmesan cheese (2 ounces)

Drop the pasta into a large pot of boiling salted water, stir once to separate and cook until al dente, about 12 minutes. Drain in a colander.

Heat the olive oil in a medium-size skillet over medium heat and sauté the garlic until lightly browned, about 1 minute. Add the tomatoes, olives and basil. Cook for 3 minutes. Add the chicken stock and cook for 3 more minutes. Season with salt and pepper.

Place the pasta in a warm bowl and toss with the sauce and Parmesan cheese.

Yield: 4 servings.
Per serving: 234 calories, 11 g protein, 29 g carbohydrates, 9 g fat (3 g saturated), 9 mg cholesterol, 271 mg sodium.

Pasta Tutto Funghi
Gino Laghi

This pasta dish comes from the Apennines in the Emilia-Romagna region of northern Italy, where I was raised and where mushroom collecting has always been a popular pastime. The autumn mushrooms are plentiful, beautiful and incredibly fragrant. They can be earthy, meaty or peppery, and the more mushroom varieties you use for this dish, the more complex the flavor.

1 large fresh portobello mushroom (about 8 ounces)
6 medium-size fresh shiitake mushrooms (about 8 ounces)
6 medium-size fresh oyster mushrooms (about 4 ounces)
1 large fresh porcini mushroom (about 4 ounces) or 2 ounces
*   dried porcini mushrooms*
2 tablespoons olive oil
4 cloves garlic, crushed
1 cup chicken stock (page 147) or canned fat-free, low-salt
*   chicken broth*
1/3 cup white wine
Salt and freshly ground pepper to taste
12 ounces fresh or dried tagliatelle, fettuccine, gnocchi or
*   pasta of your choice*
1/2 cup chopped fresh Italian parsley

Wipe and thinly slice the mushrooms. If using dried porcini, soak in warm water until tender, about 15 minutes. Reserve the soaking water. Strain it and save for your sauce.

In a large, nonstick skillet, heat the olive oil over medium heat and sauté the garlic until browned, 1 to 2 minutes. Remove and discard the garlic. Add the sliced mushrooms and sauté until cooked through and the juices are released, 5 to 7 minutes.

Add the chicken stock, white wine and reserved soaking water and cook until the sauce has thickened and reduced by one-third. Season with salt and pepper. Keep warm.

Bring a large pot of salted water to a boil. Add the pasta, stir it once or twice, and cook over medium heat until al dente, 2 to 3 minutes for fresh pasta and 8 to 10 minutes for dried pasta. Drain in a colander and add the pasta to the sauce. Toss over low heat until the pasta is well coated. Stir in the chopped parsley. Serve on warm plates.

Yield: 4 servings.
Per serving: 326 calories, 9 g protein, 56 g carbohydrates, 8 g fat (1 g saturated), 0 mg cholesterol, 473 mg sodium.

RAGOÛT OF SPICED WHITE VEGETABLES WITH PRUNE WONTONS
Mary Etta Moose

This recipe takes some time and trouble, especially if one does not already have down the basic techniques. But using techniques such as these is the only substitute I have ever found for making very low-fat dishes as complex and interesting as those that rely on fat for flavor. It should be noted that the prunes for the wontons must steep overnight in the refrigerator.

PRUNE WONTONS
4 ounces pitted prunes
1/3 cup Chardonnay wine
4 ounces low-fat ricotta cheese
Minced zest of 1 small lemon and 1 small orange
1/4 teaspoon ground coriander
Salt and freshly ground pepper to taste
24 square wonton skins

VEGETABLE BROTH
1 small fennel bulb, quartered
2 leeks (whites parts only), quartered
1 medium-size white onion, halved
4 cloves garlic, mashed
4 stalks celery, halved
1 small celery root, peeled

4 inches daikon radish
2 russet potatoes, peeled
1 strip orange peel (2 inches)
1 teaspoon coriander seeds
1 teaspoon bruised white peppercorns
8 cups water
Salt to taste

SHALLOT-SPICE MIXTURE
1 teaspoon unsalted butter
2 large shallots, minced
4 cloves garlic, minced
1 tablespoon minced fresh ginger
1 teaspoon ground ginger
1 teaspoon coriander and 1 teaspoon anise seeds, toasted and ground (page 150)

2 small slices fresh ginger
12 ounces celery root, trimmed and cut into 3/4 -inch cubes
12 ounces daikon radish, trimmed and cut into 1/2-inch cubes
8 whole shallots, bulbs separated
1 medium-size fennel bulb (12 ounces), cut into 1/2 -inch slices
4 inches thin fennel stalk, sliced into thin diagonals
2 large leeks (whites parts only), cut into 1/2-inch slices
Fresh cilantro sprigs for garnish

For the prune wontons, combine the prunes and Chardonnay in a nonreactive container, cover and let steep overnight in the refrigerator.

Mince the rehydrated prunes and combine in a small bowl with the remaining ingredients, except the wontons. Lay out wonton skins a few at a time on a work surface. Spoon 1 teaspoonful of filling in the center of each wonton, brush edges of skin with water and fold into a triangle, pressing edges closed. Take the two corners at the end of the fold, lift them toward the center and press together. Lay the wontons on a tea towel or waxed paper and cover with another towel until ready to cook.

To prepare the vegetable broth, place all the ingredients, except the salt, in a 4-quart saucepan, cover and bring to a boil. Reduce heat and simmer, partially covered, for 1 hour. Strain broth through a fine sieve lined with a double-folded cheesecloth. Return broth to pan and cook uncovered over medium heat until reduced to 1 1/2 cups. Salt to taste and set aside.

To prepare the shallot-spice mixture, melt the butter in a skillet over medium heat and sauté the shallots, garlic and fresh ginger until transparent, about 2 minutes, adding some vegetable broth as needed to prevent sticking. Add the ground ginger, coriander and anise seeds and cook 1 minute more. Set aside.

Steam the vegetables in a steamer (or in a colander set in a large covered saucepan) over simmering water containing 2 small slices of ginger. Steam the cubed celery root, daikon and shallots for 7 minutes, then add the fennel and leek slices and steam until the daikon is tender, about 3 more minutes. Transfer the hot vegetables to a bowl, toss in the shallot-spice mixture and keep warm.

Remove steamer basket, return ginger water to a boil and drop in the wontons 1 at a time. Cook wontons for 2 1/2 minutes. Drain wontons and divide among 4 warm serving bowls. Spoon spiced vegetables over wontons and ladle hot vegetable broth over all. Garnish with cilantro sprigs and serve at once.

Yield: 4 servings.
Per serving: 403 calories, 12 g protein, 82 g carbohydrates, 4 g fat (2 g saturated), 11 mg cholesterol, 364 mg sodium.

PENNE RIGATE PASTA WITH BABY ARTICHOKES AND SPINACH
Donna Katzl

This is one of those pasta dishes that makes a delightful lunch, perhaps with a simple tomato salad, or can be served for dinner with roasted or grilled chicken. It can also be made with asparagus instead of baby artichokes. I suggest slicing the asparagus into diagonal pieces. But try it first with artichokes. You'll find penne rigate pasta (small, ridged tubes with slanted edges) in most supermarkets.

10 ounces baby artichokes
6 ounces dried penne rigate pasta
2 tablespoons extra-virgin olive oil
2 to 3 cloves garlic, chopped
1/2 cup chicken stock (page 147) or vegetable stock (page 148)
2 teaspoons chopped fresh oregano
2 teaspoons grated lemon zest
1/3 cup thinly sliced scallions
2 cups washed, stemmed, drained and thinly sliced spinach (4 ounces)
Salt and freshly ground pepper to taste
3 tablespoons freshly grated Asiago cheese

Trim the stems and remove the bruised outer leaves from the baby artichokes. In a medium-size saucepan of boiling salted water, blanch the artichokes over medium heat just until tender, about 6 minutes. Cut the artichokes in half lengthwise. Set aside.

Bring a large pot of salted water to a boil, add the pasta and cook until al dente, about 12 minutes. Drain in a colander, transfer to a warm bowl, toss with 1 tablespoon olive oil and set aside.

In a 10-inch nonstick skillet, heat 1 tablespoon olive oil over medium-low heat. Add the artichokes and garlic, and sauté until lightly golden, about 3 minutes. Add the

chicken or vegetable stock, oregano, lemon zest, scallions and spinach, and cook for 3 minutes.

Transfer the skillet mixture into the bowl of warm pasta, add salt, pepper and Asiago, toss until mixed and serve.

Yield: 4 servings.
Per serving: 128 calories, 5 g protein, 16 g carbohydrates, 4 g fat (1 g saturated), 4 mg cholesterol, 250 mg sodium.

DUNGENESS CRAB RAVIOLI WITH ASPARAGUS AND ANISE BROTH
Tom Switzer

Rich foods containing ample amounts of fat, salt and sugar are the simplest way to achieve big flavor. But they can overload the senses and create a feeling of being full long before the palate is satisfied. I prefer to serve several light, clean dishes, the kind that tease the palate without surfeiting it. Here's one inspired by Chinese crab and asparagus soup. The key to the dish is a savory, anise-flavored vegetable broth and very fresh crabmeat, preferably cooked and picked yourself. Look for the truffle oil at gourmet shops and better supermarkets.

ANISE BROTH
1 tablespoon olive oil
1 bulb fennel, sliced
2 leeks (white parts only), well washed and sliced
2 medium-size yellow onions, sliced
2 carrots, sliced
4 stalks celery, sliced
4 cloves garlic, mashed
2 cups white wine (preferably Sauvignon Blanc)
6 cups water
1 tablespoon toasted anise seeds (page 150)
2 sprigs fresh thyme
1 sprig fresh rosemary

4 sprigs fresh parsley
1 bay leaf
10 black peppercorns, crushed
Salt to taste

3 live Dungeness crabs (1 ½ pounds each) or 1 pound cooked crabmeat
1 tablespoon olive oil
1 zucchini, finely chopped
2 shallots, finely chopped
1 stalk celery, finely chopped
1 carrot, finely chopped
4 fresh shiitake mushrooms (about 4 ounces), finely chopped
Salt and freshly ground pepper to taste
24 square wonton wrappers
Flour or parchment paper for preparing pan
24 asparagus, cut in half, lower halves peeled
Toasted anise seeds (page 150) and truffle oil for garnish

To prepare the anise broth, heat the oil over medium heat in a stockpot, and lightly sauté fennel, leeks, onions, carrots, celery and garlic until they sweat, about 5 minutes. Add the wine and water and add the remaining broth ingredients, except salt. Reduce heat and simmer for 1 hour. Season with salt. Strain the stock through a cheesecloth-lined strainer. Set aside.

If using live crabs instead of store-bought cooked crabmeat, handle them carefully with tongs and wash well under cold running water. Bring a large pot of salted water to a boil, carefully drop in the crabs and cook over medium heat until shells are red, 8 to 10 minutes. Rinse the crabs in cold water, drain and pick clean of meat. Set aside.

In a skillet, heat the olive oil over medium heat and sauté the zucchini, shallots, celery, carrot and mushrooms until tender, about 5 minutes. Season with salt and pepper. Let cool in a large bowl and combine with the crabmeat.

Lay out wonton wrappers a few at a time on a work surface. Place a heaping teaspoonful of the crab mixture on each wonton. Brush wonton edges with water, fold into a triangle and seal by pressing closed. Place ravioli on a baking sheet dusted with flour or lined with parchment paper. Cover with plastic wrap and set aside in refrigerator.

Just before serving time, bring anise broth to a boil in a large saucepan over medium heat, drop in ravioli and asparagus a few at a time, and cook for 2 minutes. Serve in bowls—4 ravioli and 4 asparagus each—with broth to cover. Garnish with anise seeds and a light drizzle of truffle oil.

Yield: 6 servings.
Per serving: 173 calories, 2 g protein, 18 g carbohydrates, 5 g fat (.6 g saturated), .5 mg cholesterol, 452 mg sodium.

LINGUINE WITH CHICKEN, SPINACH AND MUSTARD-DILL SAUCE
Charles Saunders

The inspiration for this dish came from a French friend who suggested that we stay home one rainy evening when we were planning to dine out. We wanted something light, easy and compatible with a Sauvignon Blanc. We used ingredients that my friend had on hand in her kitchen, including mustard, pasta, chicken and dill. The improvised dish, accompanied with a green salad and fruit tartlet, was gloriously successful.

MUSTARD-DILL SAUCE
1/2 cup water
1 teaspoon Dijon mustard
1/2 teaspoon chopped fresh dill
White pepper to taste

4 chicken legs and thighs
Salt and freshly ground black pepper to taste
1 tablespoon olive oil

1/4 cup thinly sliced red onion or leek
1/4 cup cooked white beans (optional)
1/2 cup thinly sliced Granny Smith or pippin apple
1/2 teaspoon minced lemon zest
1 tablespoon fresh dill, picked but not chopped

2 cups fresh spinach (4 ounces), well washed, stemmed and drained
8 ounces dried or fresh linguine

To prepare the mustard-dill sauce, combine the ingredients in a small saucepan. Bring almost to a boil, turn heat to low and cook, while stirring, for 1 minute. Do not allow to boil or the mustard will separate. Set aside.

Preheat the oven to 375 degrees F. Place the chicken in an ovenproof, nonstick skillet. Sprinkle with salt and pepper. Roast in the oven until juices run clear, about 30 minutes. When cool enough to handle, remove and discard skin. Remove meat from bones, slice thinly and set aside.

In a large skillet, heat olive oil, add onion or leek and optional white beans. Cook over low heat until tender, about 5 minutes. Add chicken meat, apples, lemon zest, dill and the mustard sauce. Season with salt and pepper and simmer for 2 minutes. Add spinach and cook for 1 more minute. Set aside and gently reheat just before serving.

Meanwhile, drop the linguine into a large pot of boiling salted water, stir once to separate, and cook over medium heat until al dente, about 10 minutes for dried, 3 minutes for fresh. Drain in a colander, transfer linguine to a bowl and toss with gently reheated sauce.

Yield: 4 servings.
Per serving: 327 calories, 31 g protein, 23 g carbohydrates, 11 g fat (2 g saturated), 97 g cholesterol, 126 mg sodium.

Oxtail and Potato Ravioli in Vegetable Broth
Lance Dean Velasquez

In this hearty dish, oversize ravioli are stuffed with braised oxtails, potatoes and lemon zest, and served with braising broth and thin shavings of Parmigiano Reggiano cheese for a deep-flavored, satisfying, low-fat pasta course.

1 pound disjointed oxtails, trimmed of all fat

MARINADE
1 cup dry red wine
1/2 cup dry white wine
1 teaspoon olive oil
1 carrot, sliced
1 shallot, sliced
1/2 yellow onion, chopped
1 clove garlic, mashed
1 sprig fresh thyme
1/2 bay leaf
6 black peppercorns, crushed

1 tablespoon olive oil
2 carrots, sliced
6 small boiling onions, peeled and whole
3 shallots, peeled and whole
Bouquet garni of 1 sprig fresh thyme, 1 bay leaf, 4 fresh sage leaves, 4 fresh parsley stems and 10 black peppercorns, crushed
1 1/2 cups chicken stock (page 147) or canned fat-free, low-salt chicken broth
Salt and freshly ground pepper to taste
12 cloves garlic, roasted (page 149)
8 ounces small red potatoes
1 tablespoon finely cut fresh chives
1 teaspoon minced fresh rosemary
2 teaspoons minced fresh sage

1 tablespoon finely minced lemon zest
6 ounces nonfat ricotta cheese
3 tablespoons freshly grated Parmesan cheese (preferably Parmigiano Reggiano)
36 wonton skins, or three 9 by 12-inch pasta sheets of your choice
1 egg, beaten (only if using pasta sheets)
Flour for dusting baking sheet
1 carrot, sliced
Thin shavings of Parmesan cheese, for garnish

Blanch the oxtails in a medium-size saucepan of boiling water over medium heat for 3 minutes. Drain in a colander. Combine the marinade ingredients in a nonreactive container, add the oxtails, cover and marinate in the refrigerator for 24 hours.

Preheat the oven to 350 degrees F. Strain the marinated oxtails over a bowl to catch the marinade. Reserve 1 cup marinade. Pat the oxtail joints dry with paper towels.

In an ovenproof skillet or flameproof casserole big enough to hold the oxtail joints in one layer, heat 1 tablespoon olive oil over medium heat and cook the oxtails, carrots, boiling onions and shallots until lightly browned, 5 to 7 minutes. Add the bouquet garni, stock, reserved marinade, and salt and pepper. Bring the liquid to a boil, cover pan and braise in the oven until the meat is tender, 2 to 2 1/2 hours.

Strain the braising liquid through a fine strainer into a narrow container (to make fat removal easier). Transfer oxtails to a bowl and discard braising vegetables and bouquet garni. Refrigerate braising liquid for several hours, until the fat has congealed.

Remove the oxtail meat from the bones, discarding any fat and sinew. Using a sharp knife, cut the meat into small dice, about 1/4 inch, and set aside in a medium-size bowl. Slip the roasted garlic cloves out of their skins into a small bowl and set aside.

In a medium-size saucepan, cover the potatoes with cold water, add salt and cook over medium heat until tender, about 12 minutes. Drain the potatoes, quarter them and pass them through a ricer. Then, lightly mix the potatoes with the oxtail meat.

In another bowl, fold the chives, rosemary, sage and lemon zest into the ricotta, and season with salt and pepper. Stir in the oxtail-potato mixture and the grated Parmesan. Adjust seasoning.

Lay out 18 wonton skins on a work surface or tea towel. Place a heaping teaspoon of stuffing in the center of each wonton skin. Mist the edges of the skins with water and top them with remaining 18 skins, pressing edges together. Place the ravioli on a baking sheet lightly dusted with flour and set aside. (If using pasta sheets, cut in half to 6 by 9-inch sheets, place stuffing at 3-inch intervals, brush pasta with beaten egg, top with another sheet, press closed and cut into squares.)

Just before serving time, remove the braising liquid from refrigerator, lift congealed fat from surface with a slotted spoon and transfer broth to a saucepan. Add the sliced carrot, cover and gently simmer over low heat until carrot slices are crisp tender, about 3 minutes. Keep warm, but don't allow the broth to reduce.

In a large pot of salted boiling water, drop in the ravioli one by one and cook over medium heat. When the ravioli float to the surface, in about 3 minutes, remove with a slotted spoon and drain well on paper towels. Serve 3 ravioli per portion in warm serving bowls. Add hot broth, carrot slices and roasted garlic. Garnish with Parmesan shavings and serve at once.

Yield: 6 servings.
Per serving: 255 calories, 16 g protein, 22 g carbohydrates, 6 g fat (2 g saturated), 26 mg cholesterol, 381 mg sodium.

SPICY TOFU WITH LINGUINE
Andy Wai

This recipe is an updated version of a popular old northern Chinese dish, *ma po tofu*, which I loved as a child growing up in Hong Kong. The recipe calls for a small amount of meat and hot pepper seasoning, which makes it flavorful, aromatic and especially good on a chilly evening when the pepper can really warm you up. Best of all, it's quick and easy to prepare.

SPICY MARINADE
1 cup water
3 scallions (including green parts), chopped
2 tablespoons tomato paste
1 tablespoon cornstarch
1 teaspoon Asian hot chili sauce or to taste
1 teaspoon Asian sesame oil
1 teaspoon sugar
½ teaspoon salt
¼ teaspoon toasted and crushed Sichuan peppercorns (page 150)

8 ounces soft tofu, drained and cut into ¼-inch cubes
8 ounces dried linguine or pasta of your choice
1 tablespoon olive oil
2 large cloves garlic, minced
½ pound lean ground beef or pork
1 tablespoon Chinese oyster sauce
1 teaspoon Asian sesame oil

To prepare the spicy marinade, combine all the ingredients in a medium-size bowl. Stir until the mixture is smooth. Gently fold in the tofu cubes until covered with the marinade. Set aside for 30 minutes.

In a large pot of boiling salted water, add the linguine, stir once to separate and cook until al dente, about 12 minutes or according to package directions.

Meanwhile, heat the olive oil in a heavy-bottomed, medium-size saucepan, add the garlic and ground meat and cook over high heat for 3 minutes, stirring to separate the meat chunks. Pour in the spicy marinade and tofu, bring to a boil, then reduce heat to low. Cover and cook until the sauce has thickened, 15 to 20 minutes, stirring occasionally to prevent sticking to the bottom of the pan.

When the linguine is done, drain in a colander, rinse noodles quickly under hot running water and drain well. Return linguine to the pan and toss with oyster sauce and sesame oil.

Place linguine on a warm serving platter, spoon the tofu sauce over the noodles and serve immediately.

Yield: 4 servings.
Per serving: 270 calories, 14 g protein, 23 g carbohydrates, 13 g fat (2 g saturated), 24 mg cholesterol, 300 mg sodium

RISOTTO WITH WILD MUSHROOMS AND BABY ARTICHOKES
Walter Zolezzi

When we introduced this dish at the Fly Trap, it proved so popular with our customers that it soon became part of our standard repertoire. A hearty, creamy dish, it's comfort food without being rich in fat. Be certain to use arborio rice, an Italian short-grained variety from the Po delta. It works best for risotto and is sold at better markets. If you don't have time to make your own vegetable stock, you'll find Swanson's canned vegetable broth at most supermarkets.

1 pound baby artichokes
6 cups vegetable stock (page 148) or canned vegetable broth
2 tablespoons olive oil
2 tablespoons minced shallots
1 cup minced yellow onions

12 ounces fresh wild mushrooms (such as shiitake, oyster, porcini, chanterelle), stemmed and sliced
2 cups arborio rice
1/2 cup dry white wine
Salt and freshly ground pepper to taste
Chopped fresh Italian parsley for garnish

Trim the stems and remove bruised outer leaves from the baby artichokes and cut them in half. Place them in a large, nonreactive saucepan with the vegetable stock, bring to a boil, lower heat and cook the artichokes at a simmer just until tender, 5 to 6 minutes. Using a slotted spoon, remove artichokes from broth, drain and set aside.

Bring the vegetable stock back to a boil, reduce heat to low and keep the stock hot until ready to use in the risotto.

In a large skillet, heat the olive oil, add the shallots and onions, and sauté over low heat until translucent, about 5 minutes. Add the mushrooms and sauté over medium heat until tender, about 5 minutes. Stir in the arborio rice, stirring until well coated. Add the wine and continue stirring until wine has been absorbed. Using a ladle, gradually add small amounts of hot stock, and cook each addition until almost absorbed, stirring constantly. When the rice is creamy and nearly al dente, add the baby artichokes, heat through and season with salt and pepper. The whole cooking process should take about 20 minutes. Serve garnished with chopped parsley.

Yield: 4 portions.
Per serving: 395 calories, 8 g protein, 68 g carbohydrates, 7 g fat (1 g saturated), 0 mg cholesterol, 383 mg sodium.

UDON SUKI
Maggie Waldron

A few years ago, a popular noodle shop in Beijing was reported to be sprinkling opium poppy seeds over its noodles with the hope that customers would become addicted to them.

This is an interesting marketing strategy, but noodles without opium are quite addictive enough for me. The Japanese wide noodle called *udon* is the star of this classic *suki* (variation of sukiyaki) with vegetables, clams and little pork balls. If you have a tabletop cooker, you can cook the ingredients in front of your guests.

1/2 pound lean ground pork
1 egg white, lightly beaten
1 tablespoon all-purpose flour
1 tablespoon low-sodium soy sauce
1 tablespoon grated fresh ginger
8 cups chicken stock (page 147) or canned fat-free,
*   low-salt chicken broth*
6 cups assorted vegetables (such as carrots, celery,
*   cauliflower, broccoli, daikon and/or turnips), cut into*
*   thin strips or slices*
18 clams in their shells
1 jalapeño chili, seeded and finely chopped
1 package (21 ounces) fresh udon noodles or 1 package
*   (17.6 ounces) dried*
1 tablespoon Asian sesame oil
Salt and freshly ground pepper to taste

In a small bowl, lightly mix the pork with the egg white, flour, soy sauce and ginger. Shape into 1-inch balls. In a large saucepan, bring the chicken stock to a boil. Lower heat to a simmer, add the pork balls and cook for 5 minutes. Add the vegetables, clams and jalapeño, and simmer just until the vegetables are crisp tender and the clams have opened. Remove any clams that do not open.

Meanwhile, cook the udon in a pot of boiling salted water for 3 minutes or according to package directions. Drain and toss with sesame oil. Add to the pan with the rest of the ingredients, season with salt and pepper, and heat through.

Yield: 6 servings.
Per serving: 377 calories, 31 g protein, 39 g carbohydrates, 11 g fat (2 g saturated), 49 mg cholesterol, 833 mg sodium.

POLENTA SOUFFLÉ WITH GRILLED PORCINI MUSHROOMS
Robert Helstrom

This recipe is a twist on the old Southern dish, spoon bread, in turn adapted from the way we generally do it at Kuleto's restaurant for this reduced-fat version. When fresh porcini are unavailable, you can substitute another meaty wild mushroom, such as portobello or shiitake.

3 cups low-fat milk
1 cup polenta
1/2 teaspoon salt
1 1/2 tablespoons sugar
2 egg yolks, lightly beaten
3 teaspoons baking powder
4 egg whites
Olive oil spray or olive oil for brushing
8 ounces fresh porcini mushrooms, stemmed and
*   sliced 1/4 inch thick*
Salt and freshly ground pepper to taste

Scald the milk in a large saucepan over medium heat and stir in the polenta. Cook until thick, stirring constantly, about 10 minutes. Add the salt and sugar, turn off heat and let cool slightly. Stir in the egg yolks and baking powder.

Preheat the oven to 350 degrees F. In a large bowl, beat the egg whites until stiff and fold into polenta mixture. Lightly spray or brush a 9-inch springform pan or soufflé dish with olive oil. Spoon soufflé mixture into the pan and bake in the oven until the top is puffed and golden brown, about 45 minutes.

Meanwhile, preheat the grill or broiler. Lightly spray or brush mushroom slices with olive oil, season with salt and pepper, and grill or broil them for 2 minutes per side.

Divide the soufflé into wedges and serve with mushroom slices on top.

Yield: 4 servings.
Per serving: 303 calories, 14 g protein, 40 g carbohydrates, 9 g fat (3 g saturated), 120 mg cholesterol, 675 mg sodium.

VEGETABLE CURRY WITH APPLE COUSCOUS
Christopher L. Majer

The curry dish I've chosen is both healthy and satisfying. It contains no dairy products and only a small amount of olive oil to bring out the flavor of the vegetables. The dish calls for a variety of vegetables. Choose six or more of the ones you like best, and try to use the freshest seasonal vegetables. The result will show immediately on your taste buds.

CURRY SAUCE
1 tablespoon olive oil
1/4 cup chopped yellow onion
1/4 cup chopped leek (white part only)
3 cloves garlic, minced
1/2 apple, peeled, cored and chopped
1/2 pear, peeled, cored and chopped
1/2 ripe banana, peeled and chopped
1 tablespoon rice flour or 1 teaspoon all-purpose flour
3 tablespoons curry powder (preferably Madras style) or to taste
2 1/2 cups fresh carrot juice
Salt and white pepper to taste

COUSCOUS
1 cup couscous
1 cup apple juice
Salt and white pepper to taste

SUGGESTED VEGETABLES
12 ounces small red potatoes, halved
4 ounces pearl onions
2 Japanese eggplants, diced
8 ounces green beans, trimmed
4 ounces mushrooms (caps only)
1 medium-size zucchini, sliced
1 medium-size yellow squash (such as crookneck), sliced
1/2 cup green peas (8 ounces unshelled)

To prepare the curry sauce, heat the olive oil in a nonreactive skillet over medium heat and sauté the onion, leek and garlic without coloring, about 5 minutes. Add the apple, pear and banana, and cook 5 more minutes, stirring occasionally. Mix in the flour and curry powder. Lower heat and add the carrot juice slowly, stirring frequently with a whisk. Skim off any foam that forms on the surface. Do not let the mixture boil. Cook at a gentle simmer for 10 to 15 minutes until thickened. Season with salt and pepper. Strain the mixture through a fine-mesh strainer. Set aside.

Place the couscous in a bowl. Bring the apple juice to a boil in a small saucepan, and add salt and pepper. Pour over the couscous and cover with plastic wrap. After 10 minutes, fluff up with a fork. The couscous is ready. Set aside.

In a steamer (or in a strainer set in a large covered saucepan), steam the vegetables separately over boiling water until crisp tender, about 12 minutes for the potatoes, 7 minutes for the onions, 5 to 6 minutes for the eggplant and beans, 4 minutes for the mushrooms and 2 minutes for the squash and peas. Season vegetables lightly with salt and pepper.

Assemble the dish on a large serving platter or on individual plates. Arrange the vegetables on a bed of couscous and top with curry sauce.

Yield: 4 servings.
Per serving: 356 calories, 12 g protein, 76 g carbohydrates, 3 g fat (.4 g saturated), 0 mg cholesterol, 345 mg sodium.

BOUILLABAISSE EN FOLIE
Roland Passot

GRILLED TUNA WITH VEGETABLE MIGNONETTE
David Kinch

CORIANDER-ENCRUSTED AHI TUNA WITH
VEGETABLES AND GLASS NOODLES
Elka Gilmore

BROILED MAHIMAHI ON BLACK BEANS WITH
TOMATO-MANGO RELISH
Michael Sabella

POACHED SEA BASS WITH TOMATO WATER
AND SPRING VEGETABLES
Eric Gallanter

SEA BASS BAKED IN PARCHMENT WITH
LEMON AND THYME
Kirk Webber

GRILLED STURGEON WITH CHILI-SOY SAUCE,
BABY BOK CHOY AND NORI CRISPS
Barbara Figueroa

COLD POACHED HALIBUT WITH GOLDEN PEPPER
COULIS AND PAPAYA-MINT RELISH
Gloria Ciccarone-Nehls

STEAMED HALIBUT WITH CARROTS
AND CUMIN SAUCE
Gérald Hirigoyen

entrées

HALIBUT STUFFED WITH SCALLOP MOUSSE
WITH SPICY ORANGE-GINGER SAUCE
Frances Wilson

SWORDFISH WITH EGGPLANT CAPONATA
Patrizio Sacchetto and Mark Herand

SWORDFISH WITH PINEAPPLE CHUTNEY
AND BROILED BANANA
Joel Guillon

GRILLED SALMON WITH ANCHO-SESAME
VINAIGRETTE, ROASTED BUTTERNUT SQUASH AND
BLUE-CORN TORTILLA CRISPS
Thom Fox

CHILLED SPICED SALMON WITH SHAVED FENNEL
AND BROCCOLI RABE
Kenneth Oringer

SALMON POACHED IN COURT BOUILLON WITH SALSA VERDE
Alice Waters

SALMON AL FORNO WITH WHITE BEANS
Rick Hackett

CHICKEN BREAST WITH PORCINI VINAIGRETTE
Patrizio Sacchetto and Mark Herand

STEAMED WHOLE ROCKFISH WITH BASIL AND TOMATO
Jay Harlow

MY UNCLE'S POACHED FISH
Martin Yan

GRILLED FISH IN TURKISH MARINADE OF
YOGURT, CORIANDER, CARDAMOM AND LEMON
Joyce Goldstein

BONELESS CHICKEN BREAST ROLLED OVER
WILD MUSHROOMS AND SPINACH
Hubert Keller

POULE-AU-POT UPDATED
Stanley Eichelbaum

CHICKEN AND DUMPLINGS
Narsai M. David

ROASTED PIGEON WITH
WILD RICE-POLENTA TRIANGLES
Judy Rodgers

ROAST LOIN OF PORK WITH ORANGE, RED ONION,
OREGANO AND MARSALA
Carlo Middione

VEAL NOISETTES WITH CITRUS JUICE
AND APPLE MOUSSE
Jean-Pierre Dubray

MEDALLIONS OF VENISON WITH
CARAMELIZED GREEN APPLES
Julian Serrano

WINTER VEGETABLE CASSEROLE
Narsai M. David

VEGETARIAN NAPA CABBAGE ROLLS WITH MOREL
MUSHROOMS AND TOMATO-THYME SAUCE
Donna Katzl

Bouillabaisse en Folie
Roland Passot

This is my own adaptation of bouillabaisse, the great fish stew of Marseilles. I named it for my restaurant, La Folie, where it has always been a winner. Of course, we don't have the Mediterranean fish, but we have the wonderful flavors of garlic, saffron and anise. This stew is a hearty, filling, aromatic dish, served with rouille, the traditional piquant garnish for bouillabaisse (adjusted here in a low-fat version). At home, I like to serve the stew from a soup tureen set in the middle of the table, and let everyone dig in. You don't eat just one bowlful, you make a meal of it. Since the recipe calls for lobster and crab shells and fish bones to make a broth, you'll need to talk to your fish dealer about obtaining them.

Bouillabaisse Broth
1 tablespoon olive oil
Shells from 2 lobsters or crabs
10 cloves garlic, mashed
2 medium-size yellow onions, minced
1 stalk celery, sliced
2 leeks (white parts only), well washed
1 fennel bulb, cut up
5 pounds bones of nonoily fish (such as halibut,
  John Dory or snapper)
1/2 teaspoon saffron
1 tablespoon fennel seeds
1 tablespoon anise seeds
1 tablespoon coriander seeds
Pinch of cayenne pepper
6 very ripe medium-size tomatoes, chopped
4 cups dry white wine
8 cups water or to cover

Rouille
2 cups bouillabaisse broth
Pinch of saffron
1 teaspoon minced garlic
2 cups low-fat or fat-free mayonnaise

12 mussels in their shell, scrubbed
12 clams in their shell, scrubbed
Sea salt to taste
12 sea scallops (1 ounce each)
2 pounds assorted fish fillets (such as snapper, halibut,
  grouper, perch, sea bass, rockfish or monkfish)
Diced ripe tomato and chopped fresh chives for garnish
Toasted sourdough country bread for accompaniment

To prepare the broth, in a large nonreactive saucepan or stockpot, heat the olive oil over medium heat. Sauté the lobster or crab shells for 3 to 5 minutes. Add the garlic, onions, celery, leeks and fennel, and continue to sauté until translucent, about 5 minutes. Add the fish bones, saffron, spice seeds and cayenne. Mix well and cook over low heat for 10 minutes. Add the tomatoes and wine. Bring to a boil over medium heat. Add the 8 cups water, or more to cover. Return to a boil, lower heat and simmer for 30 minutes. Strain, discarding the solids, and set aside.

To prepare the rouille, in a small saucepan, bring 2 cups of bouillabaisse broth to a boil, add the saffron and reduce the liquid over medium heat by two-thirds until quite thick, being careful not to burn it. Combine with the minced garlic and mayonnaise. Cover and refrigerate until ready to use.

In a large saucepan bring half the remaining bouillabaisse broth to a boil, season lightly with salt, add the clams and mussels and cook, covered, over medium heat until the shells open. Remove and discard any shellfish that do not open. In another saucepan, bring the other half of the broth to a boil, season lightly with salt and turn the heat very low. Add the scallops and fish pieces, and poach without boiling for 2 to 3 minutes. Do not overcook.

Divide the mussels, clams, scallops and fish pieces among 6 soup bowls. Cover with boiling broth. Garnish with diced tomato and chopped chives, and serve with rouille, along with toasted sourdough country bread.

Yield: 6 servings.
Per serving: 452 calories, 39 g protein, 34 g carbohydrates, 6 g fat (.9 g saturated), 66 mg cholesterol, 688 mg sodium.

GRILLED TUNA WITH VEGETABLE MIGNONETTE
David Kinch

This tuna dish works equally well with swordfish. If using tuna, the thicker the cut the better the recipe will work. Whether tuna or swordfish, it's important that the fish go immediately from the grill to the plate atop the vegetable mignonette. The natural juices that run out of the fish become an integral part of the sauce.

6 ounces baby green beans
1 yellow onion, finely diced
2 tablespoons drained capers
3 red bell peppers, roasted, seeded and finely diced
  (page 150)
Leaves from 2 sprigs fresh thyme, coarsely chopped
1 tablespoon chopped fresh parsley
1/2 teaspoon freshly crushed black pepper
1/2 cup fresh lemon juice
2 tablespoons olive oil, plus more for brushing fish
Salt and freshly ground pepper to taste
6 ahi tuna steaks (4 ounces each)

Blanch the green beans in a large pot of boiling water for 2 minutes, then refresh in a bowl of ice water. Drain beans and finely chop to the same size as the other vegetables.

In a medium-size nonreactive bowl, combine the green beans, onion, capers, peppers, thyme, parsley, crushed pepper, lemon juice and olive oil. Season with salt to taste and let marinate at room temperature for 2 hours. Stir occasionally.

Prepare the grill. Brush tuna steaks with olive oil and season with salt and pepper. Grill tuna to desired doneness, 1 to 2 minutes on each side for medium rare, which will allow tuna to stay moist.

Spoon vegetable mixture in a circle on warm plates and place tuna directly on top.

Yield: 6 servings.
Per serving: 235 calories, 27 g protein, 8 g carbohydrates, 10 g fat (2 g saturated), 43 mg cholesterol, 225 mg sodium.

CORIANDER-ENCRUSTED AHI TUNA WITH VEGETABLES AND GLASS NOODLES
Elka Gilmore

This dish brings together an exotic combination of Asian flavors for a wonderfully light sauce that is ideally paired with ahi tuna. And the richness of the fish is accented by the special pungent quality of the coriander. The vegetables and glass noodles are an attractive accompaniment for the dish.

GINGER-CORIANDER CONSOMMÉ
3 cups chicken stock (page 147) or canned fat-free,
  low-salt chicken broth
2 stalks lemongrass, trimmed of tough tops and outer
  layers, and sliced
2 ounces fresh ginger, finely minced
6 tablespoons coriander seeds, toasted and crushed
  (page 150)
2 tablespoons rice vinegar
2 egg whites

1 zucchini
1 yellow squash (such as crookneck)
1 carrot
6 ounces glass noodles (page 149)
1 1/2 pounds number-one grade ahi tuna fillet
Salt and freshly ground pepper to taste
Olive oil spray

To prepare the consommé, bring chicken stock to a boil in a medium-size nonreactive saucepan. Reduce heat and add lemongrass, ginger and 3 tablespoons of the coriander. Simmer for 45 minutes. Add vinegar. Strain through a fine strainer, return stock to pan and bring back to a boil. Whisk egg whites into hot stock and simmer over low heat until it becomes clear. Strain and set aside.

Cut zucchini, yellow squash and carrot into thin, noodle like strips, using a mandoline-style slicer or vegetable peeler. In a large saucepan, blanch vegetables separately in salted boiling water until tender but not limp, about 2 minutes for each vegetable. Drain and set aside. Using the same saucepan, cook the noodles in salted boiling water until softened, about 3 minutes. Drain and set aside.

Cut tuna into 3 log-shaped pieces. Roll tuna in remaining 3 tablespoons coriander and season with salt and pepper. Spray a medium-size, nonstick skillet with olive oil spray and heat over high heat. When the pan is quite hot, sear tuna on all sides, about 1 minute each side for rare. Toss vegetables and noodles in heated consommé and divide on 6 warm plates. Slice tuna into thick slices and place on top of the noodles and vegetables. Spoon on the remaining consommé.

Yield: 4 servings.
Per serving: 377 calories, 47 g protein, 16 g carbohydrates, 13 g fat (2 g saturated), 64 mg cholesterol, 842 mg sodium.

BROILED MAHIMAHI ON BLACK BEANS WITH TOMATO-MANGO RELISH
Michael Sabella

I was influenced for this simple, satisfying dish by my fondness for mahimahi, a firm, meaty, terrific-tasting Hawaiian fish, and by my love of Latin and Caribbean food. The relish is not unlike a salsa, with mango added to give it a lift. If mahimahi is unavailable, the recipe works almost as well with swordfish or snapper. Remember to start this a day ahead to allow time for soaking and marinating.

TOMATO-MANGO RELISH
1 medium-size ripe tomato, diced
1 scallion (white part only), chopped
Juice of 1 lime
1 medium-size ripe mango, peeled and diced
2 tablespoons chopped fresh cilantro

8 ounces dried black beans
1 bay leaf
1 small yellow onion, finely chopped
1 clove garlic, minced
Juice of 1 lemon
Salt and freshly ground pepper to taste
4 mahimahi fillets (6 ounces each)
Olive oil spray
Fresh cilantro sprigs for garnish

In a small nonreactive bowl, combine the relish ingredients, cover and refrigerate overnight.

Soak the black beans overnight in cold water to cover. Drain and transfer to a large saucepan. Add the bay leaf, onion, garlic and enough water to cover. (Try not to add too much water, since the finished beans should keep their shape.) Bring to a boil, reduce the heat and simmer just until the beans are tender and the water is dark and sassy, about 1 hour. Drain off excess liquid and remove bay leaf. Add lemon juice and season with salt and pepper to taste. Keep warm.

Preheat the broiler or prepare the grill. Lightly spray the mahimahi with olive oil spray and season with salt and pepper. Broil or grill the fish until it is slightly pink inside, 4 to 5 minutes on each side. Serve with the black beans underneath and the relish over the top center of the fish. Decorate the plate with cilantro sprigs.

Yield: 4 servings.
Per serving: 243 calories, 36 g protein, 13 g carbohydrates, 4 g fat (.6 g saturated), 54 mg cholesterol, 96 mg sodium.

POACHED SEA BASS WITH TOMATO WATER AND SPRING VEGETABLES
Eric Gallanter

For a low-fat entrée, this can't be beat, since the fish contains the only fat that goes into the dish. Yet it's a remarkably tasty dish. The broth is made from tomato water and it has lots of flavor—the bright, acidic savor of tomatoes. And there's also the natural appeal of the vegetables and fish. I suggest using very ripe, even over ripe tomatoes for this recipe because they're sweeter and make more juice. You'll need to start a day ahead, since the tomato water is an overnight project.

10 medium-size, very ripe tomatoes (about 3 ¹/₂ pounds)
Salt
4 sea bass fillets (5 ounces each)
8 small red potatoes (about 12 ounces), cut in half
8 baby carrots (about 6 ounces)
6 ounces haricots verts (ultrathin green beans)
12 asparagus (about 8 ounces), trimmed
³/₄ cup green peas (12 ounces unshelled)
¹/₄ cup cut-up fresh tarragon leaves
Salt and freshly ground pepper to taste

To make the tomato water, quarter the tomatoes and put them into a food processor or blender. Process for only 10 seconds until they are finely chopped but not puréed. Line a bowl with a triple thickness of cheesecloth or a white napkin. Pour in the tomatoes and tie the ends of the cloth with a string. Suspend the bag from a rack over a nonreactive bowl in the refrigerator overnight, allowing the tomato water to drip out slowly into the bowl. You should have 4 cups of tomato water.

Transfer the tomato water to a large nonreactive saucepan and heat it over medium to low heat to a simmer. Season lightly with salt, add the fish fillets and poach them, covered, in the simmering liquid just until done, 5 to 7 minutes. Remove fish and keep warm.

Reheat the tomato water over medium heat, bringing it to a boil, then lower heat and add the vegetables separately in the order of their cooking time. First, add the potatoes and carrots, which take the longest, about 7 minutes. Add the green beans and cook for 3 minutes, then the asparagus and peas for 1 minute. Lastly, add the tarragon leaves and adjust the seasoning with salt and pepper.

Serve in heated shallow soup bowls, placing the sea bass in the center and vegetables around it, with broth spooned over them.

Yield: 4 servings.
Per serving: 422 calories, 45 g protein, 52 g carbohydrates, 5 g fat (1 g saturated), 75 mg cholesterol, 335 mg sodium.

SEA BASS BAKED IN PARCHMENT WITH LEMON AND THYME
Kirk Webber

Baking fish *en papillote* (in parchment paper), is a classic method that has gained favor in today's health-conscious culinary era. It can be done virtually without fat because the parchment seals in the aroma and juices until just before eating, and the lemon zest, thyme, garlic and vegetables heighten the flavor to such an extent that you never miss the fat.

3 cloves garlic, chopped
3 shallots, chopped
Minced zest and juice of 2 lemons
$1/2$ cup chopped fresh thyme
2 tablespoons olive oil
Salt and freshly ground pepper to taste
4 sheets parchment paper (about 17 by 17 inches)
1 medium-size bulb fennel, thinly sliced
1 red bell pepper, seeded and thinly sliced
4 sea bass fillets (6 ounces each)

Combine the garlic, shallots, lemon zest and juice, thyme, olive oil, and salt and pepper in a food processor or blender and process until well mixed.

Preheat the oven to 375 degrees F. Fold the parchment sheets in half and cut into half circles. Unfold and place one-fourth of the fennel and bell pepper on the lower half of each sheet, leaving a wide margin of paper. Lay a piece of fish on top of the fennel mixture, then spoon one-fourth of the herb mixture over each fillet. Fold over the parchment and close it up, tightly crimping the paper to seal it. Place the packets on a baking sheet and bake in the oven for 15 minutes.

Serve fish immediately in parchment packets on large dinner plates, slitting them open at the table to release aroma.

Yield: 4 servings.
Per serving: 281 calories, 41 g protein, 10 g carbohydrates, 8 g fat (1 g saturated), 90 mg cholesterol, 181 mg sodium.

GRILLED STURGEON WITH CHILI-SOY SAUCE, BABY BOK CHOY AND NORI CRISPS
Barbara Figueroa

This dish has proven very popular with diners at Victor's restaurant. They like the unique, juicy texture and delicious flavor of the sturgeon, once so plentiful, but now a rarity and largely farm grown. And they like the light, spicy flavor of the sauce, which is very much part of the Pacific Rim influence in today's cuisine. You'll find the nori sheets at better supermarkets. If not, they're available at Japanese markets, along with the mixed sea vegetable salad and other Asian ingredients.

CHILI-SOY SAUCE
2 $1/4$ cups rich chicken stock (page 147)
2 tablespoons low-sodium soy sauce
$1/2$ teaspoon Asian chili sauce with garlic
1 $1/2$ teaspoons Asian fish sauce
$1/2$ teaspoon sugar
2 teaspoons potato starch
1 teaspoon butter
$1/2$ teaspoon fresh lime juice
Salt and freshly ground pepper to taste

4 sheets nori (Japanese dried seaweed)
6 heads baby bok choy
2 pounds sturgeon fillet, trimmed and cut diagonally
  into 6 portions
Olive oil or olive oil spray for coating fish
Mixed sea vegetable salad (optional) for garnish

To prepare the sauce, combine the chicken stock, soy sauce, chili sauce, fish sauce and sugar in a saucepan. Bring to a boil, lower heat and simmer mixture for 10 minutes. Dilute the potato starch in a small amount of cold water and add to the sauce, whisking constantly until lightly thickened. Remove from heat and whisk in the butter and lime juice. Correct seasoning with salt and pepper.

Cut the nori sheets into $^1/_4$-inch strips, using kitchen shears or a very sharp knife. Spread out strips, a few at a time, in a hot skillet and toast over medium heat for 1 minute, until crisp. Be careful. They burn easily.

In a steamer (or on a rack placed in a large, covered saucepan or wok) place the bok choy over boiling water and steam until tender, about 5 minutes. Season with salt and pepper.

Preheat the grill or broiler. Coat the sturgeon lightly with olive oil and season with salt and pepper. Grill or broil until the fish tests for doneness, 2 to 3 minutes on each side. It should still be barely translucent in the middle.

To serve, place the sturgeon on warm plates with the bok choy. Ladle sauce over and around the sturgeon and place a bundle of nori crisps on top. If you wish, garnish the plate with pieces of sea vegetable salad.

Yield: 6 servings.
Per serving: 284 calories, 35 g protein, 13 g carbohydrates, 9 g fat (2 g saturated), 119 mg cholesterol, 813 mg sodium.

COLD POACHED HALIBUT WITH GOLDEN PEPPER COULIS AND PAPAYA-MINT RELISH
Gloria Ciccarone-Nehls

Easy to prepare and delicious, this cold halibut dish is made in advance, has fantastic visual appeal and looks great plated or on a buffet table. It has become a summer favorite with my customers at the Big Four. For a variation on the recipe, try it with scallops or sea bass.

2 cups water
1 cup white wine
Juice of 2 lemons
Salt and white pepper to taste
6 halibut fillets (6 ounces each)

1 tablespoon canola oil
1 sheet parchment paper

GOLDEN PEPPER COULIS
2 large golden bell peppers, seeded and cut up
1 small yellow onion, coarsely chopped
1 medium-size potato, peeled and cut into 1-inch cubes
1 $^1/_2$ teaspoons grated fresh ginger
Salt and pepper
$^1/_4$ cup champagne

PAPAYA-MINT RELISH
1 tablespoon fresh ginger juice (page 149)
1 ripe papaya, peeled, seeded and diced
2 tablespoons champagne
Juice of 1 lime
$^1/_4$ red bell pepper, seeded and diced
$^1/_2$ medium-size red onion, diced
1 scallion, minced
1 tablespoon chopped fresh mint leaves
Salt and cayenne pepper to taste
$^1/_2$ teaspoon dried lavender flower or 2 teaspoons
  chopped fresh lavender

4 heads baby lettuce or 2 heads Bibb lettuce
2 Belgian endives
Snipped fresh chives for garnish

Preheat the oven to 400 degrees F. Combine the water, wine, lemon juice, salt and pepper in a shallow nonreactive baking dish. Place the halibut fillets 2 inches apart in the dish. Rub the top of the fish with canola oil and lay parchment paper over the fish. Poach the halibut in the oven until the fish is just cooked through, about 15 minutes. Let cool, then chill in the refrigerator.

To prepare the golden pepper coulis, combine all the ingredients, except the wine, in a 2-quart saucepan and simmer for 20 minutes. Purée mixture in a blender, add the wine and adjust seasoning. Cover and chill.

To prepare the papaya-mint relish, combine all the ingredients in a bowl. Let sit for an hour before using.

To serve, spread some coulis on each plate, arrange lettuce leaves and endive spears on two sides of plate, place fish in the middle and top with relish. Garnish with snipped chives.

Yield: 6 servings.
Per serving: 330 calories, 38 g protein, 20 g carbohydrates, 6 g fat (.8 g saturated), 54 mg cholesterol, 206 mg sodium.

STEAMED HALIBUT WITH CARROTS AND CUMIN SAUCE
Gérald Hirigoyen

There's nothing healthier than steamed fish. And halibut is the fish people seem to prefer for its silkiness and flavor. At Fringale, I serve the halibut with an unusual sauce made with puréed carrots and quickly braised sliced carrots. It all comes together nicely, and it could not be easier to prepare.

2 medium-size carrots, sliced as thin as possible
2 tablespoons olive oil
3 medium-size carrots, diced
1/2 medium-size yellow onion, chopped
4 cloves garlic, finely chopped
Juice of 1 lemon
Juice of 1 lime
3 cups water
1/2 teaspoon cumin seeds
Salt and freshly ground pepper to taste
2 tablespoons chopped fresh chives
2 tablespoons chopped fresh parsley
4 halibut fillets (4 ounces each)

In a saucepan of boiling water, blanch the thinly sliced carrots over medium heat for 2 minutes. Drain in a colander, then plunge into a bowl of ice water to halt the cooking process. Drain again and set aside.

Heat the olive oil in a medium-size skillet over medium heat. Add the diced carrot, onion and garlic. Cook until caramelized, 5 to 7 minutes. Add the lemon and lime juice, and cook for 1 more minute. Pour in the 3 cups of water and cumin seeds. Bring to a boil, reduce heat and simmer for 10 minutes. Season with salt and pepper.

Let the mixture cool a bit, then transfer to a blender and purée at high speed for 2 minutes. Return the blended sauce to the saucepan and add the blanched sliced carrots. Bring to a boil, reduce heat and simmer for 3 minutes. Remove from the heat, stir in the chives and parsley, and set aside.

Season the halibut fillets with salt and pepper, place them in a steamer (or on a rack placed in a large covered saucepan), and steam over boiling water until the fish is just cooked through, 2 to 3 minutes. To serve, divide the carrot-cumin sauce among 4 plates and put the steamed fish on top.

Yield: 4 servings.
Per serving: 270 calories, 26 g protein, 15 g carbohydrates, 10 g fat (1 g saturated), 48 mg cholesterol, 113 mg sodium.

Halibut Stuffed with Scallop Mousse with Spicy Orange-Ginger Sauce
Frances Wilson

Growing up in Dublin, Ireland, a Friday ritual was to walk down to the harbor to buy fish fresh off the trawlers for dinner. After considerable haggling, my mother would come away triumphant with her favorite fish—halibut. We loved its distinctive flavor and rich creamy texture. The recipe I present here came about one Sunday afternoon at Lalime's in Berkeley, when someone called the restaurant requesting a low-fat fish entrée. I was able to prepare this dish from ingredients on hand. Although the recipe may look a little daunting, it really is quick and easy to do, and also quite pleasing to the eye and palate.

Marinade
2/3 cup fresh orange juice
1 tablespoon grated fresh ginger
Grated zest of 1/2 orange
1 tablespoon rice vinegar

2 pounds halibut fillet
Salt and white pepper to taste

Scallop Mousse
4 scallions, sliced
1 tablespoon grated fresh ginger
1/2 teaspoon chopped garlic
1 pound bay scallops
1/4 teaspoon Asian chili paste with garlic
Grated zest of 1/2 orange

Orange-Ginger Sauce
2 cups fresh orange juice
1 tablespoon chopped fresh ginger
1 cup mirin (Japanese sweet rice wine)
1/8 teaspoon Asian chili paste with garlic
1 cup water

Steamed snow peas, sugar snap peas or asparagus for accompaniment

Mix together all the marinade ingredients in a medium-size nonreactive bowl. Remove any skin and bones from the halibut and cut the fish into 6 flat, even-size pieces. Season with salt and pepper, dip into the marinade and place on a plate. (Do not let the fish sit in the marinade.) Cover fish with plastic wrap and set aside in refrigerator.

To prepare the scallop mousse, place the scallions, ginger and garlic in a food processor or blender and process until finely chopped. Add the scallops, chili paste, orange zest, salt and pepper. Pulse a few times to make a smooth mixture. Do not overwork. Transfer to a bowl, cover and refrigerate.

To prepare the orange-ginger sauce, place the orange juice and ginger in a nonreactive saucepan, bring to a boil and cook over medium heat until reduced by one third. Strain out the ginger and return sauce to pan. Add the mirin, chili paste and water. Bring back to a boil, reduce heat and simmer for 5 minutes. The sauce may be prepared in advance and reheated before serving.

Place a spoonful of mousse on one half of each halibut fillet and fold the other half over it. In a bamboo or metal steamer (or on a rack placed in a large covered saucepan), place as many stuffed fillets as will fit, and steam over boiling water until the fish is firm to the touch, about 7 minutes. Repeat the process with the other fillets, if necessary.

To serve, place a stuffed fillet in the center of each plate and surround with warm sauce. Snow peas, sugar snap peas or asparagus accompany this dish very well.

Yield: 6 servings.
Per serving: 325 calories, 45 g protein, 18 g carbohydrates, 4 g fat (.6 g saturated), 73 mg cholesterol, 388 mg sodium.

Swordfish with Eggplant Caponata
Patrizio Sacchetto and Mark Herand

Caponata is a traditional dish of southern Italy and Sicily, its piquant flavor inspired by the hot climate of the region. It's served in many ways, always at room temperature and usually in an antipasto course. But at Umberto, we use caponata as a sauce for an entrée of grilled or baked swordfish, since the sweet-and-sour combination of flavors goes very well with seafood.

3 tablespoons olive oil, plus more for rubbing fish
1 medium-size eggplant (about 12 ounces), cut
  into ¼-inch dice
1 stalk celery, cut into ¼-inch dice
1 medium-size yellow onion, cut into ¼-inch dice
2 cloves garlic, minced
½ cup canned tomato purée
¼ cup chicken stock (page 147) or canned fat-free,
  low-salt chicken broth
¼ cup raisins
¼ cup toasted pine nuts (page 150)
Salt and freshly ground pepper to taste
2 large swordfish steaks (12 ounces each and ¾ inch thick)

In a large nonstick skillet, heat the olive oil over medium heat and sauté the eggplant until tender, about 7 minutes; then remove from the pan with a slotted spoon. Add the celery and sauté until tender, about 5 minutes, and remove. Add the onion and garlic, and sauté until translucent, about 5 minutes.

Return the eggplant and celery to the pan, add the tomato purée, chicken stock, raisins and pine nuts; simmer for 5 to 10 minutes. Season with salt and pepper and set aside.

Prepare a grill or preheat the oven to 400 degrees F. Cut each swordfish steak into 2 portions, rub them with olive oil and season with salt and pepper. Grill the fish until just cooked through, 2 to 3 minutes on each side, or alternatively, place in a shallow baking pan and bake in the oven for 8 to 10 minutes.

Divide caponata among 4 plates and top with swordfish.

Yield: 4 servings.
Per serving: 447 calories, 47 g protein, 22 g carbohydrates, 19 g fat (3 g saturated), 85 mg cholesterol, 365 mg sodium.

Swordfish with Pineapple Chutney and Broiled Banana
Joel Guillon

I was looking for an exotic dish that would be an adventure for guests at Cafe Fifty-Three in the ANA Hotel, so I asked my Pakistani sous-chef, Faran Turab, to think of something unusual and different. He came up with this pineapple chutney, which I put together with swordfish and broiled banana. People went wild over it and told us that they found it especially appealing because it's so low in calories and fat.

Pineapple Chutney
1 tablespoon canola oil
1 small yellow onion, finely diced
1 ounce fresh ginger, finely chopped
2 tablespoons granulated sugar
2 tablespoons white wine vinegar
1 red jalapeño chili, seeded and finely chopped
2 cups finely diced fresh pineapple
Salt to taste

2 large bananas
1 tablespoon brown sugar
4 swordfish steaks (6 ounces each)
Olive oil spray
Salt and freshly ground pepper to taste
4 thin slices fresh pineapple, cut in half

To prepare the chutney, heat the canola oil in a medium-size skillet, and sauté the onion and ginger over low heat for 5 minutes. Add the sugar and vinegar, and cook the mixture until caramelized, about 10 more minutes. Add the jalapeño and pineapple and bring to a boil over medium heat. Lower heat and simmer for 30 minutes, until most of the juice has reduced. Season with salt and set aside.

Preheat the grill or broiler. Cut the bananas in half lengthwise, leaving on the skin, and lightly coat the flesh side with brown sugar. Spray or brush the swordfish with olive oil and season with salt and pepper. Grill or broil the swordfish until just cooked through, 2 or 3 minutes on each side. Cook the banana halves, cut side down on the grill or cut side up under the broiler, for 1 minute. Grill or broil the pineapple slices for 1 minute.

To assemble, place some chutney in the center of each plate, top with swordfish and arrange a banana half and pineapple slices around them.

Yield: 4 servings.
Per serving: 373 calories, 34 g protein, 30 g carbohydrates, 12 g fat (2 g saturated), 66 mg cholesterol, 721 mg sodium.

GRILLED SALMON WITH ANCHO-SESAME VINAIGRETTE, ROASTED BUTTERNUT SQUASH AND BLUE-CORN TORTILLA CRISPS
Thom Fox

Since I moved to San Francisco in 1985, the salmon season has always given me a great sense of excitement and joy. The quality of the Pacific Coast salmon, its flavor and texture are unsurpassed. It's definitely one my favorite fish to cook and serve friends. And a recipe such as this goes exceedingly well with a Pinot Noir from the Napa-Sonoma Carneros district.

2 medium-size butternut squash (about 1 ¼ pounds each), cut in half lengthwise, with seeds scooped out and saved
1 teaspoon walnut oil
2 tablespoons prepared horseradish
2 teaspoons white wine vinegar
Salt and freshly ground pepper to taste

ANCHO-SESAME VINAIGRETTE
8 ancho chilies, split open and seeded
⅓ cup sherry vinegar
3 tablespoons sugar
1 teaspoon Asian sesame oil
2 tablespoons olive oil
¾ cup chicken stock (page 147) or canned fat-free, low-salt chicken broth
2 tablespoons toasted sesame seeds (page 150)
Salt to taste

4 blue corn tortillas
Olive oil spray
6 salmon fillets (6 ounces each)

Preheat the oven to 375 degrees F. Brush the squash halves lightly with walnut oil, place cut side down in a baking pan and lay the seeds out alongside the squash to toast for use later as a garnish. Roast in the oven until squash flesh is very soft when pierced with a fork, about 30 minutes. Remove squash and seeds from oven and let rest until cool enough to handle.

Pick seeds clean of fiber and set aside. Scoop out squash flesh and purée in a food processor or blender with horseradish and vinegar. Scrape down the sides of the processor bowl, season with salt and pepper, and purée until smooth. Transfer purée to a shallow baking dish for later reheating.

To prepare the vinaigrette, heat a small dry skillet over medium heat and toast the ancho chilies until they blister, about 2 minutes, taking care not to scorch them. Place the toasted chilies in a bowl of hot water and let rest for 20 minutes. Drain chilies and purée in a food processor or blender, adding a little olive oil, if needed, to help make the purée smooth. Press chili purée through a fine strainer to remove any tough skin and leftover seeds. In a nonreactive bowl, whisk together the chili purée and the remaining vinaigrette ingredients. Taste for seasoning and set aside.

Preheat the oven to 400 degrees F. Cut the blue corn tortillas into thin strips. Coat lightly with olive oil spray. Spread out the strips on a baking sheet and toast in the oven until crisp, 5 to 7 minutes. Place squash purée in oven and reheat for 10 minutes, stirring occasionally.

Preheat the grill or broiler. Brush or spray the salmon with olive oil and season with salt and pepper. Grill or broil salmon until fillets reach a nice medium-rare stage inside, about 3 minutes on each side.

To assemble dish, place a scoop of squash purée and a salmon fillet on each plate. Spoon vinaigrette over the salmon and garnish with toasted squash seeds and crisp tortilla strips.

Yield: 6 servings.
Per serving: 420 calories, 37 g protein, 30 g carbohydrates, 17 g fat (2 g saturated), 93 mg cholesterol, 275 mg sodium.

CHILLED SPICED SALMON WITH SHAVED FENNEL AND BROCCOLI RABE
Kenneth Oringer

Italians are very fond of eating broccoli rabe with lemon, and the combination of flavors gives this dish its distinction. The broccoli is crisp and pleasantly bitter, and the lemon is sharp and refreshing. The contrast of flavors works as a foil to cut through the richness of the salmon.

2 salmon fillets (4 ounces each)
1/2 teaspoon caraway seeds
1/2 teaspoon coriander seeds, toasted and crushed (page 150)
Salt and freshly ground pepper to taste
1 tablespoon curry oil (page 149)
1 small bulb fennel
1 tablespoon fresh lemon juice
2 tablespoons extra-virgin olive oil
1 tablespoon chopped fresh chives
1 small red onion, thickly sliced
*6 ounces broccoli rabe, larger stems well trimmed
    and peeled of thick skin*
1/2 teaspoon red pepper flakes
Snipped fresh chives for garnish

Season the salmon with caraway seeds, coriander, salt and pepper. In a medium-size nonstick skillet, heat the curry oil and sauté the salmon over medium heat until medium rare, 2 to 3 minutes each side. Remove salmon to a plate, let cool somewhat, cover with plastic wrap and set aside in the refrigerator to chill.

Shave the fennel with a mandoline-style slicer or a sharp knife. In a small bowl, toss the fennel with lemon juice, 1 tablespoon of the olive oil, salt, pepper and chopped chives. Set aside.

Preheat the grill or broiler. Grill or broil the red onion slices on both sides until soft, about 5 to 7 minutes. Set aside.

In a saucepan, blanch the broccoli rabe in boiling salted water over medium heat for 3 minutes. Remove and plunge into a bowl of ice water to refresh, then drain. In a skillet, heat 1 tablespoon olive oil and sauté broccoli rabe, red onion and red pepper flakes over medium heat for 2 minutes.

To serve, arrange the salmon with broccoli rabe and red onion on 2 plates. Top with shaved fennel and garnish with snipped chives.

Yield: 2 servings.
Per serving: 382 calories, 28 g protein, 23 g carbohydrates, 21 g fat (3 g saturated), 62 mg cholesterol, 667 mg sodium.

SALMON POACHED IN COURT BOUILLON WITH SALSA VERDE
Alice Waters

Salmon for poaching is best cut from the section of the fish closest to the head. This part is moist, meaty and finely flaked. The tail section is much leaner and tends to go dry in a poaching liquid. Court bouillon is an aromatic bath of herbs and vegetables. Its flavors combine with the salmon to make a delicate soup. The salsa verde acts as a condiment, creates a forceful taste and enhances the flavor of the salmon greatly.

SALSA VERDE
4 anchovy fillets (preferably Italian salt-packed)
1 small shallot, minced
3 tablespoons extra-virgin olive oil
2 tablespoons chopped fresh Italian parsley
1 tablespoon drained capers, rinsed and finely chopped
1 teaspoon white wine vinegar
1 teaspoon chopped fresh tarragon
1 teaspoon chopped fresh oregano
1 teaspoon chopped fresh thyme
1 small clove garlic, minced
Salt and freshly ground pepper to taste

COURT BOUILLON
3/4 cup very thinly sliced yellow onion or leeks
2/3 cup very thinly sliced carrot rounds (2 small carrots)
1/3 cup very thinly sliced celery (1 stalk)
4 sprigs fresh thyme (preferably lemon thyme)
2 large sprigs fresh Italian parsley
3/4 cup dry white wine (such as Sauvignon Blanc)
5 cups water
Salt to taste

2 pounds salmon fillet (1 inch thick), cut into 6 portions

To make the salsa verde, soak the anchovy fillets in cold water in a small bowl for 15 minutes, changing the water several times. Drain and squeeze out moisture. Chop anchovies finely. Place in a small bowl and stir in the remaining salsa ingredients. Taste and adjust seasoning with salt, pepper and additional vinegar, if necessary. It should be slightly tart. Set aside.

To make the court bouillon, place the ingredients in a nonreactive pot wide enough to hold the salmon pieces comfortably. Bring to a simmer, cover and cook over medium-low heat for 20 minutes. Taste and add salt, if needed.

Maintain the court bouillon at a bare simmer. Add the salmon and poach just until the flesh is opaque, about 5 minutes. Transfer the salmon to warm soup bowls and ladle court bouillon and vegetables into each bowl. Top with a spoonful of salsa verde and serve.

Yield: 6 servings.
Per serving: 243 calories, 23 g protein, 4 g carbohydrates, 12 g fat (2 g saturated), 64 mg cholesterol, 388 mg sodium.

SALMON AL FORNO WITH WHITE BEANS
Rick Hackett

This rustic recipe for oven-baked salmon is one of my favorites because I love baked fish, and I especially like the combination of fish and white beans, which is very Italian. You can prepare the beans by soaking overnight or by using the quick-soak method, which I prefer and indicate in the recipe. The dish gets a great response from my customers at Enrico's, served with aioli drizzled over the salmon. For this reduced-fat version, I've omitted the aioli.

1 1/2 cups (9 ounces) dried white beans
1 whole carrot
1/2 yellow onion
1 stalk celery
1 bay leaf
1/3 cup diced yellow onion
1/3 cup diced carrot
1/3 cup diced celery
2 tablespoons olive oil
3 cloves garlic, minced
2 large ripe tomatoes, peeled, seeded and diced
1/2 cup white wine
8 medium-size prawns, peeled, deveined and diced
4 salmon fillets (6 ounces each)
Salt and freshly ground pepper to taste
Chopped fresh parsley for garnish

Place the beans in a large saucepan with water to cover. Bring to a boil over high heat, then turn off heat and let them soak, covered, for 1 hour. Drain the beans, return to pan and add clean water to cover. Add the whole carrot, 1/2 onion, celery stalk and bay leaf. Bring to a boil, reduce heat, and cook, covered, at a simmer until the beans are tender, about 1 1/2 hours. Drain the beans. Remove and discard the carrot, onion, celery and bay leaf. Reserve 1 to 2 cups of the cooking liquid.

In a small saucepan of boiling salted water, blanch the diced onion, carrot and celery over medium heat for 2 minutes. Drain and set aside.

Preheat the oven to 400 degrees F. In a large, nonreactive, ovenproof skillet or Dutch oven, heat the olive oil over medium heat and sauté the garlic until it begins to color. Add the tomato and cook for 1 minute. Add the cooked beans, blanched diced vegetables, white wine, 1 cup of the reserved bean cooking liquid and the prawns. Bring to a boil. Lay the salmon fillets on top of the bean mixture and season with salt and pepper. Place skillet in the oven and bake until salmon is medium rare, about 5 minutes.

When the salmon is removed from the oven, you can adjust the brothiness of the dish to your preference by adding more heated bean cooking liquid. Serve in bowls with salmon on top, garnished with chopped parsley.

Yield: 4 servings.
Per serving: 575 calories, 46 g protein, 36 g carbohydrates, 18 g fat (2.8 g saturated), 115 mg cholesterol, 406 mg sodium.

entrées

109

Chicken Breast with Porcini Vinaigrette

Patrizio Sacchetto and Mark Herand

We took a classical chicken and mushroom dish from Italy's Piedmont district and eliminated the cream and heavy reduction sauce. We lightened it up with a vinaigrette and turned it into a summery dish. It's our interpretation of a chicken dinner made into a salad main course. Shiitakes may be substituted for the porcini, which are harder to find fresh.

6 boneless and skinless half chicken breasts
Leaves from 6 sprigs fresh lemon thyme
Salt and freshly ground pepper to taste
6 cups (10 ounces) mixed baby salad greens
2 tablespoons extra-virgin olive oil
1 clove garlic, mashed
3 cups (12 ounces) sliced fresh porcini mushrooms
3 tablespoons chopped fresh Italian parsley
4 Roma (plum) tomatoes, peeled, seeded and diced
3 tablespoons balsamic vinegar
2 tablespoons raspberry vinegar

Preheat the oven to 400 degrees F. Place the chicken breasts in a roasting pan, season with thyme, salt and pepper. Bake in the oven for 15 minutes. Remove chicken and let rest for 5 minutes. Reserve pan juices.

Divide salad greens among 6 plates. Thinly slice chicken and place on top of salad.

In a medium-size skillet, heat the olive oil over medium heat. Add the garlic and brown about 1 minute. Remove garlic, add mushrooms and sauté for 5 minutes. Add parsley and tomatoes, cook 2 minutes, add reserved pan juices and vinegar, and cook 2 more minutes. Season with salt and pepper. Spoon mushroom mixture over chicken and greens, and serve.

Yield: 6 servings.
Per serving: 232 calories, 29 g protein, 14 g carbohydrates, 6 g fat (1 g saturated), 68 mg cholesterol, 102 mg sodium.

Steamed Whole Rockfish with Basil and Tomato

Jay Harlow

This is one of my favorite Western adaptations of an Asian cooking technique. In place of the ginger and scallions typical of a Chinese steamed fish, it uses Mediterranean flavors of tomato, garlic and herbs. And whereas the Chinese version might be finished with a little aromatic sesame oil, this version uses fragrant extra-virgin olive oil.

1 whole rockfish (such as rock cod, snapper or similar fish,
   about 2 pounds)
Salt and freshly ground pepper to taste
Grated zest of 1/2 lemon
1 large ripe tomato, peeled, seeded and roughly chopped
2 cloves garlic, thinly sliced
1/2 cup fresh basil leaves or 1 to 2 sprigs fresh
   marjoram or thyme
1 tablespoon extra-virgin olive oil

Have the fish cleaned and scaled, with the head and tail left on. Open the belly cavity and pull away any remaining bits of organs. Rinse thoroughly and pat dry. Extend the belly cavity by cutting from the vent back toward the tail. Score both sides of the fish with diagonal slashes almost to the bone every inch or so. Season the fish lightly inside and out with salt and pepper.

Place the fish on a heatproof plate in an upright "swimming" position, spreading out sides to keep it upright. Bend the tail around if necessary to fit on the plate. Scatter the lemon, tomato, garlic, and basil over the fish, tucking a basil leaf into each cut in the sides.

Set up a wok or other large covered pan with a steaming rack, and add water to an inch below the rack. Cover the wok and bring the water to a rolling boil. Remove the lid, opening it away from you to prevent burns, and place the fish plate on the rack. Cover and steam until a skewer easily enters the thickest part of the fish, 15 to 20 minutes. Just before serving, drizzle the olive oil all over the fish.

Yield: 2 servings.
Per serving: 322 calories, 51 g protein, 7 g carbohydrates, 9 g fat (1 g saturated), 122 mg cholesterol, 163 mg sodium.

MY UNCLE'S POACHED FISH
Martin Yan

When I was a young boy in Guangzhou, China, my uncle and I would wake up before dawn to catch some big fish in the local river. Most of the time our tiring efforts were unsuccessful, and we ended up telling stories about the fish that got away. But often, we came back with a wonderful catch and my uncle would cook the fish more or less in this way. If you are not a fisherman, visit your local fish market. Any white fish will taste good in this dish.

4 slices ginger, crushed
1 scallion (including green part), lightly crushed
Salt to taste
1 ¹/₂ pounds firm whitefish fillet (such as cod, halibut or sea bass) cut into 4 pieces, about ³/₄ inch thick

SAUCE
1 tablespoon canola oil
1 teaspoon minced fresh ginger
¹/₃ cup rice vinegar
3 tablespoons catsup
2 tablespoons low-sodium soy sauce
3 tablespoons packed brown sugar
¹/₂ teaspoon hot pepper sauce or Asian chili oil
2 teaspoons cornstarch dissolved in 4 teaspoons water

1 scallion (including green part), cut into 1 ¹/₂-inch slivers for garnish

Pour 2 inches of water into a wok or other pan large enough to hold the fish. Add the ginger, crushed scallion and salt, and bring to a boil. Reduce the heat to low. Add the fish, cover, and simmer until the fish turns opaque, 6 to 8 minutes. Lift the fish out with a slotted spoon. Drain it briefly, transfer to a serving platter and keep it warm.

While the fish is cooking, prepare the sauce. Heat a medium-size saucepan over high heat until hot. Add the canola oil, swirling to coat the surface. Add the ginger and cook, stirring, until fragrant, about 10 seconds. Add the rice vinegar, catsup, soy sauce, brown sugar and hot pepper sauce, and mix well. Add the cornstarch solution and cook, stirring, until the sauce boils and thickens, about 30 seconds. Pour the sauce over the fish and garnish with scallion slivers.

Yield: 4 servings.
Per serving: 236 calories, 31 g protein, 16 g carbohydrates, 4 g fat (.5 g saturated), 73 mg cholesterol, 490 mg sodium.

GRILLED FISH IN TURKISH MARINADE OF YOGURT, CORIANDER, CARDAMOM AND LEMON

Joyce Goldstein

Low-fat or nonfat yogurt makes a great marinade for fish or chicken. The yogurt tenderizes as it seasons. Serve this fish with rice pilaf and steamed spinach or broiled eggplant and peppers with walnut coriander pesto.

YOGURT MARINADE
1 cup low-fat or nonfat plain yogurt
1 tablespoon coriander seeds, toasted and ground (page 150)
½ teaspoon ground cardamom
Salt and freshly ground pepper to taste
3 tablespoons fresh lemon juice

6 fillets (5 ounces each) of a firm whitefish (such as cod, halibut, flounder, sea bass or swordfish)
Olive oil for brushing
Salt and freshly ground pepper to taste
Chopped fresh dill and lemon wedges for garnish

Combine all the marinade ingredients in a shallow non-reactive dish. Add the fish fillets, spoon some marinade over them, cover and marinate in the refrigerator for 4 to 6 hours.

Preheat the grill or broiler. Brush excess marinade from fish. Brush fish lightly with olive oil. Sprinkle with salt and pepper. Grill or broil fish until cooked through, about 4 minutes on each side. Serve garnished with chopped dill and lemon wedges.

Yield: 6 servings.
Per serving: 159 calories, 17 g protein, 4 g carbohydrates, 3 g fat (.7 g saturated), 63 mg cholesterol, 104 mg sodium.

BONELESS CHICKEN BREAST ROLLED OVER WILD MUSHROOMS AND SPINACH

Hubert Keller

Here's an unusual method of poaching chicken. It's rolled in plastic wrap to conserve the natural juices and heighten the flavor. In July, 1993, I had the honor to be the first guest chef ever to go to the White House and do a presentation on low-fat food. I included this chicken recipe in the dinner menu I served on Bastille Day to President and Mrs. Clinton and their daughter Chelsea. It was certainly a big day in my life.

2 pounds chicken bones, necks and wings
1 small carrot, diced
1 small yellow onion, diced
½ stalk celery, diced
1 clove garlic, mashed
1 cup dry white wine
1 ripe tomato, coarsely chopped
5 cups water
Bouquet garni of 1 bay leaf, 2 sprigs fresh thyme and 3 sprigs fresh parsley
1 bunch spinach (about 12 ounces)
2 teaspoons olive oil
Salt and freshly ground pepper to taste
½ pound fresh wild mushrooms (black chanterelles, shiitakes, morels, even truffles), wiped clean and sliced
4 large boneless and skinless half chicken breasts
4 10-inch squares plastic wrap
1 tablespoon port wine
1 teaspoon hazelnut oil

Preheat the oven to 375 degrees F. Place the chicken bones in a baking pan and roast in the oven until they are golden brown, about 40 minutes. Add the carrot, onion, celery and garlic, and continue roasting for 10 minutes. Remove the grease with a spoon and pour in the white wine. Add the tomato and roast until the liquid is reduced by half, about 7 more minutes.

Transfer roasted ingredients to a stockpot. Add the water and bouquet garni, bring to a boil and skim off the scum that rises to the top. Lower the heat to barely simmering and cook uncovered for 1 hour, skimming periodically. (The more you skim, the clearer your stock will be.) Pour the stock through a sieve. Discard the solids and return the stock to the pot. Skim off the fat and cook the stock over medium heat until reduced to a $^1/_2$ cup. Set aside.

Remove the spinach stems completely and wash the leaves carefully. Heat a large skillet over medium heat with 1 teaspoon of the olive oil and then add the spinach, stirring until the leaves are wilted but still bright green, 2 to 3 minutes. Season with salt and pepper. Drain and cool in a colander, then squeeze out all the moisture with your hands. Set aside.

In a medium-size skillet, heat 1 teaspoon olive oil over medium heat and sauté the mushrooms until they begin to exude liquid, about 5 minutes. Season with salt and pepper. Set aside.

Remove the tendons from the chicken breasts and discard. Flatten each breast lightly with a large knife. Season with salt and pepper on both sides. Place on top of each chicken breast a tablespoon of wild mushrooms and an equal amount of wilted spinach. Then roll up each breast in a 10-inch square of plastic wrap and tie firmly with kitchen string at both ends.

Bring 4 quarts of water to a boil in a large pot, reduce the heat to a simmer and slowly lower the chicken breasts into the water. Poach them for 12 minutes. Remove them from the water and keep warm.

To prepare the sauce, in a small saucepan, bring the reserved $^1/_2$ cup of stock to a boil over medium heat. Add the port wine, cook 1 minute, stir in the hazelnut oil and adjust the seasoning.

Remove the chicken breasts from the plastic wrap. Slice them diagonally and serve with the hazelnut-flavored sauce.

Yield: 4 servings.
Per serving: 261 calories, 30 g protein, 12 g carbohydrates, 5 g fat (.8 g saturated), 68 mg cholesterol, 398 mg sodium.

POULE-AU-POT UPDATED
Stanley Eichelbaum

Poule-au-pot (chicken in the pot) was my mother's favorite comfort food. But her rendition of the classic dish was so undistinguished (and overcooked) that it took me years to appreciate it as anything more than boiled chicken. Here's a sprightly, updated version with a skinless chicken poached just until it's done and a broader gamut of herbs and aromatic vegetables to brighten and enhance the flavor.

1 chicken (about 3 pounds)

POACHING LIQUID
$^1/_2$ small yellow onion, diced
1 clove garlic, minced
2 leeks (white parts only), well cleaned and thinly sliced
2 small carrots, diced
2 stalks celery, thinly sliced
1 small fennel bulb, thinly sliced
1 medium-size turnip, diced
1 small parsnip, diced
Bouquet garni of $^1/_2$ lemongrass stalk (trimmed of tough parts and chopped), 2 sprigs fresh thyme, 4 fresh parsley stems, 1 bay leaf, 2 cloves, 8 black peppercorns, tied in cheesecloth
5 cups chicken stock (page 147) or canned fat-free, low-salt chicken broth
$^1/_2$ cup dry white wine

2 ripe tomatoes, peeled, seeded and diced
1 jalapeño chili, seeded and minced
1 cup cooked brown rice
$^1/_2$ cup fresh corn kernels (scraped from 1 ear of corn)
Salt and freshly ground pepper to taste
Chopped fresh chervil or parsley for garnish

Remove the skin from the chicken, except for the first two joints of the wings, which are hard to skin. Cut these off and save for stock. Trim off any fat that adheres to the flesh. Truss the chicken. Place it in a stockpot and add cold water to cover. Bring to a boil over high heat until scum forms on surface. Remove from heat and pour off scum and water, draining the chicken in a colander.

Rinse the pot, then return the chicken to pot and add all the ingredients for the poaching liquid. Cover and bring to a boil over high heat, turn heat to low and poach in simmering liquid for 20 minutes. With a large spoon, skim off any fat from the surface of the poaching liquid. Remove bouquet garni. Add the tomatoes, jalapeño, rice and corn. Season with salt and pepper. Cook for 3 more minutes. Test chicken for doneness by inserting a small knife in wing joint; it should be cooked through.

Transfer the chicken to a platter, remove trussing string and cut the chicken into serving pieces. Serve chicken and vegetables in soup bowls, ladle hot broth over them and garnish with chopped parsley.

Yield: 4 servings.
Per serving: 481 calories, 52 g protein, 42 g carbohydrates, 8 g fat (2 g saturated), 130 mg cholesterol, 205 mg sodium.

CHICKEN AND DUMPLINGS
Narsai M. David

With so much talk about the comfort food of yesteryear, I looked around for an old idea that could be updated and came up with this chicken and dumplings which is honestly lower in fat. I recommend skinning the whole chicken first before disjointing it, as it's much easier than trying to skin the individual pieces. And it exposes the pockets of fat behind the thighs so they can be trimmed away more easily.

1 chicken (about 3 ¹/₂ pounds), skinned and disjointed
2 cups chicken stock (page 147) or canned fat-free,
*   low-salt chicken broth*
1 ¹/₂ tablespoons cornstarch
¹/₂ cup white wine
1 large yellow onion, cut into chunks

DUMPLINGS
1 cup all-purpose flour
¹/₄ teaspoon ground allspice
2 teaspoons baking powder
¹/₄ teaspoon salt
²/₃ cup low-fat milk
2 scallions, finely minced

3 carrots, cut diagonally into 1-inch slices
1 green bell pepper, seeded and cut into strips, ¹/₄ inch
*   by 1 ¹/₂ inches*
1 teaspoon crumbled dry tarragon leaves
Salt to taste
¹/₄ to ¹/₂ teaspoon red pepper flakes
¹/₄ cup chopped fresh parsley

Place the chicken legs, thighs, wings (and back, if used) into a 5- to 6-quart Dutch oven. Add chicken stock. Stir cornstarch into wine until dissolved, then stir into pot. Stir in onion, cover pot and simmer for 20 minutes.

entrées

115

While chicken is simmering, make the dumpling batter. In a small mixing bowl, stir together the flour, allspice, baking powder and salt. Add the milk and scallions, and stir only long enough to mix the batter. Cut each chicken breast into 3 or 4 parts and add to the pot. Also add the carrots, bell pepper, tarragon, salt, pepper and parsley. Stir to distribute ingredients evenly in the pot. Spoon dumpling batter into the pot in 8 small mounds, using 2 large spoons. Cover the pot and simmer without uncovering for 20 minutes.

To serve, ladle broth into 4 soup bowls, along with chicken pieces and 2 dumplings per person.

Yield: 4 servings.
Per serving: 500 calories, 57 g protein, 40 g carbohydrates, 9 g fat (2 g saturated), 160 mg cholesterol, 640 mg sodium.

Roasted Pigeon with Wild Rice-Polenta Triangles
Judy Rodgers

Pigeon (or squab) is my favorite bird, simply roasted pink with no exotic seasonings. It is naturally rich in flavor, and if lightly cured in sea salt beforehand, it needs no added fat to produce a perfectly succulent roast. Pigeon is especially delicious with crisp, nutty wild rice-polenta triangles, which are prepared with a minimum of fat, yet are completely satisfying. Be sure to select fresh whole squab with heads, feet and wing joints attached, since you'll need the trimmings to make a sauce. You should also have homemade chicken stock, which is preferable to canned chicken broth. And note that the birds need to be cured in sea salt at least a day before roasting.

4 squab (about 14 ounces each)
Sea salt to taste
4 cups cold chicken stock (page 147)
1/2 small sweet onion (such as Vidalia or Maui), thickly sliced
1 medium-size carrot, thickly sliced
1 piece celery (about 4 inches)
1 bay leaf
4 black peppercorns
1 small sprig fresh thyme
Sea salt and freshly ground pepper to taste
1/2 cup wild rice
1 1/2 cups water
1 tablespoon dried currants
1 cup polenta (the coarsest-grained you can find)
4 1/2 cups water
2 tablespoons extra-virgin olive oil

Preheat the oven to 400 degrees F. Trim the squab. Cut off and reserve the heads, feet and first two joints of wings. Sprinkle the trimmed squab all over with sea salt. Refrigerate in a covered container for at least one day before roasting. Place the reserved trimmings in a baking pan and roast in the oven until golden brown, about 30 minutes.

When the trimmings are browned, scrape them into a heavy, nonreactive saucepan along with any caramelized pan drippings they may have exuded. Add the cold chicken stock (lacking that, add cold water and a raw chicken leg). Bring to a boil over medium heat, lower heat to a simmer and skim to remove foam from surface. Add the onion, carrot, celery, bay leaf, peppercorns and thyme. Simmer gently for 2 hours. The flavor will be at its best when the stock is still golden. Strain promptly. (Do not allow the stock to sit on the bones.) Let stock settle completely, skim off fat, and re-strain if necessary. Taste. If the flavor seems thin, you should add a second batch of vegetables, this time cut somewhat smaller, which you will strain out once they have contributed their flavor during reduction.

To reduce the stock, return it to a clean saucepan and, over low heat, simmer gently until reduced by three-fourths, to a syrupy consistency, skimming off the impurities as they accumulate at the edge of the pot. Adjust seasoning with salt and pepper. Cool, cover and then refrigerate until ready to use.

Prepare the wild rice: Simmer the rice in 1 $^1/_4$ cups lightly salted water in a covered small saucepan over low heat until tender and the grains start to burst, approximately 45 minutes. You may need to add water near the end of cooking. Add the dried currants. Drain the rice and currants, and set aside.

Prepare the polenta: In a medium-size saucepan, simmer the polenta in 4 $^1/_2$ cups water over low heat, stirring regularly. Season with salt and pepper. Allow 45 minutes for the polenta to thicken and become tender.

Heat the olive oil in a medium-size heavy skillet, add the cooked rice and sauté briefly over medium heat, about 2 minutes. Combine the rice with the cooked polenta and spread this mixture in a $^3/_4$-inch layer on a baking sheet. Cover with plastic wrap and refrigerate until firm.

About 45 minutes before serving, preheat the oven to 400 degrees F, or prepare a hot fire on your grill. Cut the hard polenta into neat, 1-inch triangles. Roast or grill the pigeons, surrounded but not crowded by the polenta for approximately 17 minutes, turning everything once to brown evenly. Season with pepper. Since the birds have been cured with salt, they probably won't need more salt.

Heat the reduction sauce gently. Allow the birds to rest 3 to 5 minutes before serving, then cut in half, bathe in sauce and garnish with the wild rice-polenta triangles.

Yield: 4 servings.
Per serving: 461 calories, 38 g protein, 34 g carbohydrates, 15 g fat (4 g saturated), 151 mg cholesterol, 820 mg sodium.

ROAST LOIN OF PORK WITH ORANGE, RED ONION, OREGANO AND MARSALA
Carlo Middione

Cooking technique can help flavor food enough so that the addition of fat is not necessary. For instance, if you caramelize certain fruits and vegetables, either by sautéing them without fat in a nonstick pan or by roasting them in the oven, you get pretty tasty results because the natural sugars scorch, thereby intensifying their flavors. Here is a dish that's delicious and should satisfy people whether they can have fat or not. I hope it will be fun to cook and puts the mind at ease.

2 large navel oranges
Pork loin (2 $^1/_2$ pounds), trimmed of fat
4 large cloves garlic, peeled and crushed to a paste
3 tablespoons dried oregano
Sea salt and freshly ground pepper to taste
2 large red onions, sliced about $^1/_4$ inch thick
$^3/_4$ cup dry Marsala wine

OPTIONAL ACCOMPANIMENTS
Boiled small red potatoes, rolled in finely chopped garlic,
  fresh basil and mint
$^1/_2$ cup brown sugar mixed with $^1/_4$ cup balsamic vinegar

Using a zester or grater, remove the zest from the oranges and set aside. Then, with a small sharp knife, peel the oranges, cut the fruit into $^1/_4$-inch slices and set aside.

Preheat the oven to 350 degrees F. Wipe the pork loin with a paper towel and put it into a shallow roasting pan. Rub the meat all over with the orange zest, then the crushed garlic, oregano, sea salt and plenty of pepper. Let the meat rest for about 30 minutes, rubbing it a couple of times to redistribute the flavorings.

Place the orange slices over the top of the pork and scatter the onions all around it. Roast the pork for about 1 hour and 20 minutes (to 140 degrees F internal temperature). After 20 minutes of roasting, slide the orange slices off the

roast and mix them well with the sliced onions. Scatter on salt and pepper. After another 20 minutes of roasting, turn over the orange and onion mixture. Sprinkle half the Marsala on the roast and mixture, and roast for another 20 minutes. Then, add the remaining Marsala.

When the roast is done, remove it from the oven and let it rest for 15 minutes. Cut it into serving slices and spoon on some of the orange and onion mixture, with any pan juices that may have developed.

The roast will go well with boiled small red potatoes rolled in finely chopped garlic, basil and mint. If you must have additional flavor, you can add as a condiment to the roast, served on the side, $1/2$ cup or more brown sugar mixed with $1/4$ cup balsamic vinegar. If it is too thick, add some warm water to make a honeylike consistency.

Yield: 6 servings.
Per serving: 425 calories, 58 g protein, 9 g carbohydrates, 13 g fat (4 g saturated), 148 mg cholesterol, 88 mg sodium.

VEAL NOISETTES WITH CITRUS JUICE AND APPLE MOUSSE
Jean-Pierre Dubray

Here is a nice departure from the classic recipe of veal with apples flambéed with Calvados. The apple mousse brings exceptional lightness to the dish, and the ginger contributes an interesting new flavor. Since it serves ten persons, it would make a spectacular dinner party entrée.

2 oranges
3 limes
Salt, freshly ground pepper and paprika to taste
1 tablespoon honey
4 cups rich veal stock (page 147)

APPLE MOUSSE
10 Granny Smith apples, cored but not peeled
4 egg whites
4 ounces low-fat ricotta
3 tablespoons grated fresh ginger

30 veal medallions or noisettes (2 ounces each), trimmed
  of fat and sinews
3 tablespoons olive oil

Using a zester, remove the zest of the oranges and limes in finely julienned strands. Blanch the zest in a small saucepan of boiling water for 2 minutes. Drain, then season the zest with salt, pepper and paprika. Set aside. Squeeze the juice from the oranges and limes. Set aside.

To prepare the citrus sauce, combine the honey, veal stock, orange juice and lime juice in a small saucepan. Bring to a boil and cook over medium heat until reduced by one-third. Set aside.

To prepare the apple mousse, slice a small piece off the top of the apples, and, with a melon baller, scoop the meat from the apples without breaking the skin. Dig out as much meat as you can and reserve the shells. Place the apple meat and half the orange and lime zest in a saucepan and cook, covered, over low heat until tender, about 10 minutes. Press the apple meat through a food mill or strainer into a large bowl.

Preheat the oven to 375 degrees F. In the bowl of an electric mixer or with a whisk, beat the egg whites to soft peaks. Then, fold the beaten egg whites, ricotta cheese and ginger into the sieved apple meat. Season with salt and pepper, and gently mix. Fill the reserved apple shells with the apple mousse and place in a baking dish. Bake in the oven for 10 minutes.

Meanwhile, season the veal with salt and pepper. Heat the olive oil in a large skillet and sauté the veal noisettes over medium-high heat until they are golden brown, 2 to 3 minutes on each side. Remove from pan to warm plates.

To serve, place a mousse-filled apple in the middle of each plate, with 3 noisettes around it. Spoon heated sauce over the noisettes. Sprinkle with remaining zest.

Yield: 10 servings.
Per serving: 379 calories, 38 g protein, 33 g carbohydrates, 10 g fat (2 g saturated), 140 mg cholesterol, 670 mg sodium.

MEDALLIONS OF VENISON WITH CARAMELIZED GREEN APPLES
Julian Serrano

I devised this dish for people who are fond of red meat but are concerned about fat and cholesterol. My customers at Masa's like it so much that it's become a very big seller. I use venison from New Zealand and it could not be lower in fat. And the clean, delicate flavor goes especially well with caramelized apples.

18 medallions of venison (2 ounces each), cut from a saddle (about 6 pounds), bones and meat scraps reserved
3 tablespoons olive oil
1 tablespoon tomato paste
1 small yellow onion, chopped
2 carrots, chopped
1 stalk celery, chopped
Bouquet garni of 1 sprig fresh thyme, 1 sprig fresh rosemary, 4 fresh parsley stems, 1 bay leaf, 1 tablespoon juniper berries and 1 tablespoon black peppercorns
10 cups water
2 shallots, chopped
2 cups red wine
1/2 cup port wine
Salt and freshly ground pepper to taste
18 baby carrots
36 asparagus tips
5 Granny Smith apples, cored and cut into eighths
2 tablespoons powdered sugar
2 tablespoons butter

After deboning and trimming the saddle, cut the bones into small pieces and use with the meat scraps to make a brown stock. Place the bones and scraps in a large, heavy-bottomed, nonreactive saucepan with 1 tablespoon of the olive oil and sauté over medium heat until they're a nice dark brown color, about 10 minutes. Add the tomato paste, onion, carrots and celery and sauté until vegetables are lightly browned, about 5 minutes. Drain off the oil from pan. Add the bouquet garni and the water and bring to a boil. Lower heat and simmer for 1 hour. Pass the stock through a fine strainer, discarding solids.

In another nonreactive saucepan, add the shallots, red wine and port, and cook over medium heat until the liquid is almost gone. Add the reserved brown stock to the wine reduction and cook over low heat for 40 minutes. Pass through a fine strainer and season with salt and pepper. Set aside.

In a medium-size saucepan of boiling salted water, blanch the baby carrots for 2 minutes, then the asparagus for 1 minute. Drain and keep warm.

In a skillet, heat the remaining 2 tablespoons of olive oil over high heat and sauté the venison medallions for about 1 minute on each side for medium rare, and transfer to a heated plate. Dust the apple pieces with powdered sugar. In another skillet, melt the butter over medium heat and sauté the apple pieces until brown, about 25 seconds on each side.

To serve, place 3 medallions like flower petals pointing out from the center of each plate. Ladle some sauce over the medallions. Between the outer edges of each medallion, place 2 pieces of apple curving outward like wings. Between the arch of the apples, place a baby carrot inside 2 asparagus tips.

Yield: 6 servings.
Per serving: 511 calories, 43 g protein, 33 g carbohydrates, 15 g fat (5 g saturated), 154 mg cholesterol, 311 mg sodium.

WINTER VEGETABLE CASSEROLE
Narsai M. David

Traditional root vegetables that used to be so common in winter dishes are much less utilized now that international shipping keeps spring vegetables available the year round. I based this vegetarian meal on an interesting mixture of root vegetables that I particularly like. Using my mother's traditional blend of garlic, onions, basil and tomato, it produces the kind of home cooking that I grew up with. Serve it as a main course or with a fish or meat entrée.

TOMATO SAUCE
1 tablespoon olive oil
2 medium-size yellow onions, sliced
3 to 4 cloves garlic, minced
¼ to ½ teaspoon red pepper flakes
1 tablespoon dried basil
2 cups (15-ounce can) diced tomatoes with the juice
2 cups (15-ounce can) tomato sauce
1 cup white wine, chicken broth or water
Salt to taste

ROOT VEGETABLES
2 medium-size rutabagas (about 1 ½ pounds)
1 small celery root (about 1 pound)
3 medium-size potatoes (about 1 pound)
2 to 3 parsnips (about 1 pound)
4 to 5 medium-size carrots (about 12 ounces)

In a large nonreactive skillet, heat the olive oil and sauté the onions over medium heat, stirring frequently, until lightly browned, about 6 minutes. Add the garlic, pepper flakes and basil. Stir for 1 or 2 minutes. Add the tomatoes and juice, tomato sauce and wine or other liquid. Season sauce with salt and remove from heat.

Preheat the oven to 350 degrees F. Peel and cut all the root vegetables into ¼-inch slices. Spread 1 cup of the sauce in a 9 by 13-inch baking dish and top with a layer of

rutabagas. Alternate sauce and remaining vegetables, ending with parsnips and carrots together on the top layer. Spoon remaining sauce over it. Cover the baking dish with aluminum foil and bake in the oven for 40 minutes. Uncover and continue baking until vegetables are tender, about 40 minutes more.

Yield: 6 servings.
Per serving: 300 calories, 7 g protein, 59 g carbohydrates, 3 g fat (.4 g saturated), 0 mg cholesterol, 723 mg sodium.

VEGETARIAN NAPA CABBAGE ROLLS WITH MOREL MUSHROOMS AND TOMATO-THYME SAUCE
Donna Katzl

Being of Polish heritage, I love cabbage rolls and was brought up on the kind that were filled with beef, pork or lamb. But I have a daughter who's a vegetarian, so I worked out this dish in deference to her. Morels or other dried mushrooms add intense flavor to the dish, but you can use fresh morels or shiitakes.

1 ounce dried morel mushrooms
1 cup boiling water
1 large head napa cabbage (about 2 pounds)
1 1/2 tablespoons olive oil
3 cups chopped yellow onions (about 2 large onions)
2 teaspoons chopped garlic
3 medium-size carrots, cut in half lengthwise and thinly sliced
Salt and freshly ground pepper to taste
2 tablespoons chopped fresh thyme or 2 teaspoons dried thyme
1 can (15 ounces) chopped tomatoes with the juice
Chopped fresh parsley for garnish
Cooked white or brown rice for accompaniment

Place the dried mushrooms in a bowl and pour 1 cup of boiling water over them. Soak for 30 minutes. Drain, reserve 1/2 cup of soaking liquid and thinly slice the mushrooms. Set aside.

To prepare the cabbage, remove 12 of the best outer leaves, trim the ends, and blanch the leaves in a large saucepan of boiling water over medium heat for 2 minutes. Drain and pat dry with paper towels. Thinly slice enough of the remaining cabbage to measure 1 cup. Set aside.

In a nonstick skillet, heat the olive oil over medium heat, add the onions, sliced cabbage and garlic, and cook, stirring frequently, for 5 minutes. Add the rehydrated mushrooms, reserved mushroom liquid and 1 cup of the carrots, and cook, stirring frequently, for 5 minutes, until carrots are just tender. Remove from heat, season with salt and pepper, and stir in 1 tablespoon of the fresh thyme.

Spoon 1/3 cup of the vegetable mixture into the center of a cabbage leaf. Fold the sides of the leaf toward the center, then roll up leaf and place seam side down in a 12-inch non-reactive skillet. Repeat with the remaining cabbage leaves and filling. Pour the tomatoes and juice over the cabbage rolls. Sprinkle with remaining carrots and thyme, and lightly season with salt and pepper. Bring to a boil over medium heat, reduce heat, cover and simmer until cabbage is tender, about 10 minutes.

Serve 2 cabbage rolls per person, garnished with chopped parsley. Can be served with white or brown rice.

Yield: 6 servings.
Per serving: 158 calories, 5 g protein, 29 g carbohydrates, 4 g fat (.5 g saturated), 0 mg cholesterol, 550 mg sodium.

side dishes and relishes

HAND-SHREDDED EGGPLANT WITH SESAME SEEDS
Bruce Cost

RATATOUILLE RONDELLI
Alain Rondelli

BORN-AGAIN MASHED POTATOES WITH YOGURT CHEESE
Judith Ets-Hokin

CRANBERRY AND PINEAPPLE CHUTNEY
Charles Saunders

PEACH, BLACKBERRY AND CASSIS COMPOTE
Lenore Nolan-Ryan

ROASTED TOMATO CHUTNEY
Joey Altman

✳

HAND-SHREDDED EGGPLANT WITH SESAME SEEDS
Bruce Cost

This banquet-style dish is a specialty of Shanghai. It's meant to be served as a salad course with one or two other cold items. It's delicious, but a few mouthfuls should suffice, as it's full flavored and rich tasting. It may also be served piled on a thin crouton. Make an effort to buy *shao hsing* wine for this dish. Available in Asian markets, it's aged for at least ten years and is more like sherry than white wine. Drink it warm, as you would sake.

2 large eggplants (1 pound each)
3 tablespoons low-sodium soy sauce
2 tablespoons cider vinegar
2 tablespoons sugar
Pinch salt
2 tablespoons shao hsing *rice wine or dry sherry*
1 tablespoon peanut oil
1 tablespoon minced fresh ginger
4 cloves garlic, minced
1 tablespoon Asian sesame oil
1 tablespoon sesame seeds, toasted (page 150)
Lettuce leaves (optional) for accompaniment

In a bamboo or metal steamer (or on a rack placed in a large covered saucepan), steam the eggplants over boiling water for 20 minutes. Remove to cool. They should be slightly collapsed.

In a small bowl, combine the soy sauce, vinegar, sugar, salt and wine. Heat the peanut oil in a small saucepan over medium heat and add the ginger and garlic. Cook a few minutes until fragrant; stir in the soy sauce mixture and sesame oil and bring just to a boil. Remove from the heat and cool.

When the eggplants are cool enough to handle, pull them apart into shreds. If the skin is tender, shred it with a knife and add it. Set aside until ready to serve.

Just before serving, place the eggplant in a colander and drain away the liquid that has accumulated around the eggplant. Transfer to a bowl, add the sauce to the eggplant and toss to combine. Sprinkle with the sesame seeds and serve on lettuce as a salad, or by itself as an appetizer.

Yield: 6 servings.
Per serving: 120 calories, 2 g protein, 16 g carbohydrates, 5 g fat (.8 g saturated), 0 mg cholesterol, 520 mg sodium.

RATATOUILLE RONDELLI
Alain Rondelli

Here is a ratatouille that's crunchy, brightly flavored and visually appealing. It avoids the mushy consistency and muddled flavor, so often found in ratatouille, by removing the inner flesh from the eggplant and zucchini and holding down the cooking to just a few minutes. It's fine as a vegetable course, and it perfectly complements fish, like sautéed petrale sole and grilled or roasted chicken.

1 medium-size eggplant
2 zucchini
1 red bell pepper
1 yellow bell pepper
3 tablespoons olive oil
1 large yellow onion, diced
Salt and freshly ground pepper to taste
10 medium-size Roma (plum) tomatoes, peeled, seeded
  and diced
1 teaspoon chopped garlic
1/2 teaspoon chopped fresh thyme

Quarter the eggplant. Scoop and discard the inner flesh, leaving only 1/4 inch of flesh close to the skin. Dice the eggplant into 1/4-inch cubes. Repeat the procedure with the zucchini.

Remove the stems, seeds and ribs from the bell peppers. Cut the peppers into ¹/₄-inch cubes.

Heat the olive oil in a large, nonreactive, ovenproof skillet. Add the onion and bell peppers and sauté over medium heat for 2 to 3 minutes. Lightly season with salt. Remove to a colander set over a bowl, letting the oil drain into it. Return the oil to the skillet. Add the eggplant and zucchini, and sauté over medium heat for 2 to 3 minutes. Season lightly with salt. Remove eggplant and zucchini to colander. Drain off the oil and return it to the skillet. Add the tomatoes, garlic and thyme, and sauté over medium heat for 3 to 4 minutes.

Preheat the oven to 350 degrees F. Combine all the vegetables in the skillet and adjust seasoning, adding pepper. Cover the skillet with a lid or aluminum foil and place in the oven for 5 to 10 minutes just before serving.

Yield: 6 servings.
Per serving: 95 calories, 2 g protein, 13 g carbohydrates, 5 g fat (.6 g saturated), 0 mg cholesterol, 366 mg sodium.

BORN-AGAIN MASHED POTATOES WITH YOGURT CHEESE
Judith Ets-Hokin

This reduced-fat version of old-fashioned mashed potatoes is flavorful, filling and satisfying. It's made with yogurt cheese, a nonfat, high-calcium alternative to sour cream, crème fraîche and cream cheese. Note that the yogurt cheese must be prepared a day ahead.

2 cups low-fat, gelatin-free plain yogurt
2 pounds russet potatoes, unpeeled
¹/₂ cup nonfat milk
3 tablespoons olive oil
Sea salt to taste
¹/₂ teaspoon Hungarian paprika
¹/₂ teaspoon white pepper

To prepare the yogurt cheese, place yogurt in a colander lined with 4 layers of cheesecloth. Set colander over a bowl to catch the liquid whey. Refrigerate covered, and allow yogurt to drain for about 24 hours, until it is reduced by half. Yogurt cheese may be stored for several days in the refrigerator in a covered container.

Cut the potatoes into pieces and cook in boiling water until tender, about 20 minutes. Drain the potatoes and mash, sieve them or put them through a food mill. Combine potatoes with yogurt cheese and remaining ingredients in the bowl of an electric mixer and beat until smooth and well mixed. Correct seasoning. Reheat gently when ready to serve.

Yield: 8 servings.
Per serving: 133 calories, 5 g protein, 27 g carbohydrates, .2 g fat (.1 g saturated), 1 mg cholesterol, 50 mg sodium.

CRANBERRY AND PINEAPPLE CHUTNEY
Charles Saunders

This chutney is so brightly flavored and different that it greatly surpasses the traditional cranberry sauce that we've grown up with. It's light, crisp and easy to make. It keeps for many days in the refrigerator, perks up a main course and is also wonderful as an accompaniment to a sandwich. It's a perfect complement for roast turkey or pork, and delicious with grilled fish or even steamed shellfish.

³/₄ cup sugar
¹/₂ cup water
1 pound fresh or frozen cranberries
¹/₄ cup toasted macadamia nuts (page 150),
   coarsely chopped
1 medium-size pineapple, peeled, cored and medium diced
2 oranges, peeled, seeded and diced
¹/₄ cup finely diced red onion
1 jalapeño chili, seeded and finely diced
¹/₄ cup coarsely chopped fresh cilantro
¹/₄ cup fresh lime juice
1 tablespoon light rum
Salt and freshly ground pepper to taste

   Bring the sugar and water to a boil in a medium-size, heavy-bottomed saucepan. Add the cranberries and bring to a boil, then lower heat and cook covered at a simmer until the cranberries have popped, 6 to 8 minutes. Drain the cranberries in a colander over a bowl, reserving the liquid and berries. Return the liquid to the saucepan and cook over medium heat until reduced to ³/₄ cup. Allow it to cool.
   Place the juice in a large nonreactive bowl, add the berries and all the other ingredients, and stir. Let it stand for several hours. Serve chilled or at room temperature.

Yield: 3 ¹/₃ cups or ten ¹/₃-cup servings.
Per serving: 138 calories, .9 g protein, 28 g carbohydrates, 2 g fat (.4 g saturated), 0 mg cholesterol, 26 mg sodium.

PEACH, BLACKBERRY AND CASSIS COMPOTE
Lenore Nolan-Ryan

When the fruit season is at its peak and ripe peaches and berries are available, nothing beats this summer compote. It's delicious with desserts like angel food cake and exceptionally good with savories like chicken, rabbit or duck.

4 pounds medium-size ripe peaches (nectarines or apricots
   may be substituted)
³/₄ cup white wine
¹/₂ cup powdered sugar
2 cups blackberries (or your favorite berry)
¹/₄ cup black currant or raspberry vinegar
¹/₄ cup crème de cassis liqueur
Salt and freshly ground pepper to taste

   Cut the peaches in half, remove pits and slice the peaches in eighths. In a large nonreactive saucepan, poach the peaches in the white wine over low heat, sifting in the powdered sugar, until fruit is tender, about 15 minutes. Remove from heat, let cool for 15 minutes and add the blackberries, vinegar and cassis liqueur. Mix gently and lightly season with salt and pepper.

Yield: about 2 quarts or ten ³/₄-cup servings.
Per serving: 106 calories, 1 g protein, 20 g carbohydrates, 0 g fat (0 g saturated), 0 mg cholesterol, 54 mg sodium.

✳

ROASTED TOMATO CHUTNEY

Joey Altman

Chutney makes simple foods like grilled fish or poultry exciting, adventurous and exotic. This chutney has a rich, deep flavor that provides another dimension to grilled or roasted entrées. Try it with salmon, mahimahi, chicken breast or, if you're up to it, rack of lamb.

2 pounds Roma (plum) tomatoes
1 teaspoon olive oil
2 tablespoons minced fresh ginger
6 cloves garlic, thinly sliced
1 teaspoon mustard seeds
1/2 teaspoon coriander seeds
1 medium red onion, cut into julienne strips
2 cups malt vinegar
1 tablespoon brown sugar
3 jalapeño chilies, seeded and minced
2 tablespoons chopped fresh cilantro
Juice of 1 lime
Salt and freshly ground pepper to taste

    Preheat the oven to 275 degrees F. Cut the tomatoes in half, remove seeds and place in a baking pan. Lightly coat with the olive oil and roast in the oven for 1 1/2 hours. Let the tomatoes cool, pull off skins and set aside.

    In a medium-size, heavy-bottomed, nonreactive saucepan, place ginger, garlic, mustard and coriander seeds, red onion, vinegar and brown sugar, bring to a boil, then cook over medium heat until reduced almost to a syrup, about 15 minutes.

    Mix in the tomatoes, jalapeños, cilantro and lime juice. Season with salt and pepper. Let sit at room temperature for 2 hours. Serve with grilled fish or chicken.

Yield: about 3 cups or twelve 1/4-cup servings.
Per serving: 50 calories, 1 g protein, 11 g carbohydrates, 1 g fat (.2 g saturated), .4 mg cholesterol, 131 mg sodium.

CHOCOLATE ESPRESSO DECADENCE
Rebecca Ets-Hokin

FRUIT SPONGE CAKE AND SUMMER PUDDING
Flo Braker

MARCY'S CHOCOLATE TRIFLE
Lenore Nolan-Ryan

QUINCE AND PEAR WHOLE WHEAT CRÊPES
WITH BLUEBERRY SAUCE
Peter DeMarais

PEARS IN BEAUJOLAIS
Roland Passot

FRUIT NAPOLEON WITH FROZEN RASPBERRY YOGURT
Kenneth Oringer

GUILT-FREE COOKIES
Barbara Karoff

PINK GRAPEFRUIT MERINGUE
WITH RASPBERRIES AND HAZELNUTS
David Coyle

MINTED CITRUS COMPOTE
Lindsey Shere

CRANBERRY SOUP WITH FRESH FRUIT
David Kinch

CHOLESTEROL-FREE RASPBERRY SOUFFLÉ
Gary Danko

GAZPACHO FRUIT SOUP
Roland Passot

RICOTTA AL CAFFÈ
Carlo Middione

CHARDONNAY SORBET
Gérald Hirigoyen

Chocolate Espresso Decadence
Rebecca Ets-Hokin

The challenge of creating a luscious low-fat dessert lies in replacing fat with some other flavor. In this dense chocolate cake, I use puréed prunes for a creamy texture, and vanilla, espresso and raspberry vinegar for a very intense, rich flavor.

1/2 cup (4 ounces) pitted prunes
1 cup brandy
1 cup nonfat milk
1 cup granulated sugar
6 tablespoons safflower oil
1 tablespoon raspberry vinegar
1 tablespoon vanilla powder or vanilla extract
1 1/4 cups unbleached all-purpose flour
2/3 cup (2 ounces) cocoa powder (preferably Dutch-processed)
1 tablespoon instant espresso powder
1 tablespoon baking soda
Parchment paper
1/4 cup powdered sugar
1 1/2 cups (10 ounces) fresh raspberries
2 tablespoons superfine sugar
1 teaspoon fresh lemon juice

In a small nonreactive saucepan, cook the prunes with the brandy over medium heat, covered, until the brandy has been absorbed and the prunes are very soft, about 20 minutes. Let cool.

Place the prunes in a food processor or blender and purée until very smooth. Add the milk, granulated sugar, safflower oil, vinegar and vanilla and process until just mixed.

Sift together the flour, cocoa, espresso powder and baking soda. Add this to the prune mixture and process until just barely smooth, about 10 seconds.

Preheat the oven to 350 degrees F. Line the bottom of a 9-inch nonstick springform pan with parchment paper. Pour the batter into the pan and bake in the oven for 40 minutes. Allow to cool on a rack.

When the cake is completely cool, remove from pan and dust with powdered sugar. Place 23 raspberries on top of the cake. In a food processor or blender, purée the remaining berries with the superfine sugar and lemon juice. Serve each slice of cake with puréed raspberry sauce.

Yield: 12 servings.
Per serving: 275 calories, 3 g protein, 40 g carbohydrates, 7 g fat (.9 g saturated), .3 mg cholesterol, 220 mg sodium.

Fruit Sponge Cake and Summer Pudding
Flo Braker

Tailor this fruit sponge cake to any season. In summer, use raspberries, blueberries or coarsely chopped figs; in fall, cranberries; and in winter, raisins or coarsely chopped dried apricots or dates. For an exceptional treat, use the cake for a summer sponge pudding (recipe follows).

1 1/2 cups sifted cake flour
1 cup sugar
1 teaspoon baking powder
1/4 teaspoon salt
3 egg yolks
1/4 cup fresh orange juice
6 egg whites
1 teaspoon cream of tartar
1 teaspoon vanilla extract
1 teaspoon finely grated orange zest
1/2 cup fresh raspberries or blueberries,
  at room temperature

Adjust the rack to the lower third of the oven and preheat the oven to 325 degrees F. Sift the flour, 2 tablespoons of the sugar, the baking powder and salt onto a sheet of waxed paper. Set aside.

In a small bowl, using an electric hand mixer, whip the egg yolks with 1 tablespoon of the sugar until mixture is thick and pale in color. Add the orange juice and continue to whip until thickened, about 4 minutes.

In the bowl of a heavy-duty electric mixer fitted with the whisk attachment, whip the egg whites just until frothy. Add the cream of tartar and continue to whip until soft peaks form. Add 1/2 cup sugar in a steady steam and continue whipping until thicker, stiffer, glossy peaks form, about 2 to 3 minutes. Whip in the vanilla.

Pour the yolk mixture and the orange zest over the egg white meringue. Fold the two mixtures together with a rubber spatula. With a metal spatula or spoon, scoop a third of the flour mixture and sprinkle it over the surface, folding with the rubber spatula. Repeat 2 more times, folding just until the ingredients are incorporated.

Gently pour about one third of the mixture into an ungreased 10-inch tube pan with removable bottom (such as an angel food pan). Sprinkle berries over the batter. Pour remaining batter over the berries. With the rubber spatula, level the surface. Bake in the oven until the top springs back slightly when lightly touched, 37 to 39 minutes.

Remove the cake from the oven and invert it over a long-necked bottle to cool for 45 minutes. To remove the sponge from the pan, slip a flexible metal spatula down one side of the pan and slowly release the cake sticking to pan. When the sides are free, push up on the removable bottom to release the cake. To loosen the removable bottom, tilt the cake and gently tap the bottom against the counter. Cover the cake with a rack and invert.

Yield: 12 servings.
Per serving: 140 calories, 3 g protein, 27 g carbohydrates, 1 g fat (.4 g saturated), 53 mg cholesterol, 112 mg sodium.

SUMMER SPONGE PUDDING
This pudding must be refrigerated for eight to twenty-four hours before serving.

1 fruit sponge cake (preceding recipe)
2 cups each fresh ripe strawberries and raspberries
4 ripe fresh figs
1 cup sugar
1 tablespoon kirsch or other eau-de-vie
1 cup low-fat plain yogurt sweetened with
  1 tablespoon honey
Chopped fresh mint for garnish

Cut 1/2-inch slices from the sponge cake. Line the sides of a 1 1/2-quart metal or ceramic bowl with cake slices, overlapping slightly, and press edges together. Cut more cake for the bottom. Fill in the gaps with small pieces of cake so the inside of container is completely covered. Set aside.

Slice the strawberries and figs, and combine with the raspberries and sugar in a heavy, nonreactive saucepan. Cook over very low heat just until the sugar dissolves and the fruit juices flow, about 4 minutes. Cool mixture for 20 minutes. Add the liqueur to the fruit and spoon it into the cake-lined container, reserving some of the juice for serving time. Cover the pudding with remaining cake slices. Set a plate on top that fits snugly inside the container. Place a 2-to-3-pound weight (such as large, unopened cans) on top and refrigerate the pudding for at least 8 hours, or up to 24 hours. Unmold it onto a serving plate, garnish with fresh berries and serve with reserved juice and dollops of yogurt sweetened with the honey. Garnish each serving with fresh mint.

Yield: 8 servings.
Per serving: 364 calories, 7 g protein, 78 g carbohydrates, 2 g fat (.9 g saturated), 81 mg cholesterol, 191 mg sodium.

Marcy's Chocolate Trifle
Lenore Nolan-Ryan

This chocolate trifle was developed by Marcy Marsh, who works with me at Ryan's restaurant on creating low-fat and nonfat desserts. The trifle is made by layering bite-size pieces of a very low-fat chocolate cake with a nonfat yogurt and cream cheese sauce, a fruit sauce and sliced fresh fruit. It's festive and delicious, and the fat content is negligible, so you and your guests can enjoy it without guilt.

Chocolate Cake
1 cup sifted all-purpose flour (measured after sifting by
  spooning into measuring cup and leveling)
⅓ cup cocoa powder
1 teaspoon baking soda
1 teaspoon baking powder
½ cup fat-free egg substitute
1 ⅓ cups packed brown sugar
⅔ cup nonfat plain yogurt (liquid whey poured off)
1 teaspoon vanilla extract

Fruit Sauce
1 pint fresh or frozen strawberries or raspberries
  (4 ripe peaches or 2 ripe mangoes may be substituted)
2 to 3 tablespoons granulated sugar
½ teaspoon fresh lemon juice

Yogurt Sauce
3 tablespoons nonfat plain yogurt
1 teaspoon vanilla extract
3 tablespoons granulated sugar
2 tablespoons Cognac, bourbon or rum
12 ounces nonfat cream cheese

4 cups assorted sliced fruit (such as kiwifruit, nectarines,
  peaches, mangoes and/or berries)
Fresh mint sprigs for garnish

To prepare the cake, preheat the oven to 350 degrees F. In a small bowl, mix together the sifted flour, cocoa, baking soda and baking powder. In a large bowl or an electric mixer fitted with a paddle, mix until very smooth the egg substitute, brown sugar, yogurt and vanilla. Fold in the flour mixture and mix thoroughly. Pour the batter into an 8 by 8-inch cake pan, either nonstick or sprayed with vegetable oil. Bake for about 30 minutes, until a toothpick inserted in the center comes out clean. Let cool, remove from pan and set aside on a wire rack.

To prepare the fruit sauce, in a blender, purée all the sauce ingredients. If using raspberries, press the puree through a fine strainer to remove seeds.

To prepare the yogurt sauce, use a food processor or electric mixer fitted with a paddle. Blend together the yogurt, vanilla, granulated sugar and liquor. Add the cream cheese in 4 or 5 stages, blending well after each addition. (Note: If you want to burn off the alcohol in the liquor, use 5 tablespoons liquor and boil in a small saucepan until reduced by half before adding to the sauce.)

To assemble the trifle, use parfait or wine glasses, alternating layers of cake, cut into 1-inch cubes, with fruit sauce, yogurt sauce and sliced fruit. Garnish with mint sprigs.

Yield: 10 servings.
Per serving: 286 calories, 11 g protein, 87 g carbohydrates, 1 g fat (.3 g saturated), 5 mg cholesterol, 366 mg sodium.

QUINCE AND PEAR WHOLE WHEAT CRÊPES
WITH BLUEBERRY SAUCE
Peter DeMarais

Here's an elegant, distinctive recipe for low-fat dessert crêpes. The filling is made with quinces, the delicious, delicately flavored autumn fruit. They're like hard, yellowish apples, not ready to be eaten until they're cooked. In this recipe, they're combined with pears for a unique flavor effect.

QUINCE AND PEAR FILLING
3 medium-size ripe quinces
3 medium-size ripe but firm pears
¼ cup granulated sugar
¾ cups water
2 tablespoons quince or pear eau-de-vie
¼ cup dried blueberries or currants
1 teaspoon grated lemon zest

CRÊPE BATTER
1 cup (8 ounces) nonfat egg substitute
1 cup whole wheat flour
1 cup low-fat milk
1 tablespoon granulated sugar
Pinch of salt

BLUEBERRY SAUCE
4 cups fresh or frozen blueberries
2 cups water
½ cup granulated sugar
2 tablespoons fresh lemon juice

Vegetable oil spray
2 cups low-fat ricotta cheese mixed with
  2 tablespoons honey
Powdered sugar for dusting

Peel the quinces, cut them into quarters and remove the cores. Cut the quarters into 1-inch pieces. Peel, quarter and core the pears, and cut them into 1-inch pieces. In a heavy-bottomed, nonreactive saucepan, bring the sugar and water to a boil, add the quinces and eau-de-vie, turn the heat to low and simmer until quinces are glossy and tender, about 10 minutes, or more if quinces are not fully ripe. Add the pears, dried blueberries and lemon zest, and simmer until pears are tender, about 5 minutes. Drain off excess liquid and set aside.

To prepare the crêpe batter, combine all the ingredients in a large bowl and whisk together. Let batter stand for at least 1 hour.

To prepare the blueberry sauce, combine the blueberries, water, sugar and lemon juice in a nonreactive saucepan and bring to a boil. Turn heat to low and simmer until reduced by half. Set aside to cool.

To make the crêpes, use a 6-inch nonstick skillet or crêpe pan. Spray the pan lightly with vegetable oil. Heat the pan over high heat. When hot, remove from heat and add about 2 tablespoons well-stirred crêpe batter. Tilt and roll the pan to coat the bottom (the thinner the crêpe, the better). Return the pan to the heat and loosen the edges of the crêpe with a plastic or rubber spatula. Cook until the underside is lightly browned. Turn the crêpe with the spatula and brown the other side. Transfer the crêpe to a plate, and repeat the procedure with remaining batter, piling up finished crêpes on 2 plates. You should end up with 20 crêpes.

To assemble, place a heaping tablespoon of quince-pear filling on each crêpe. Top with a heaping tablespoonful of ricotta-honey mixture. Roll up crêpes and lay them side by side on a baking sheet. When ready to serve, preheat the oven to 450 degrees F. Place crêpes in oven until crisp and heated through, about 5 minutes. Dust them with powdered sugar. Serve 2 crêpes per portion surrounded by blueberry sauce.

Yield: 10 servings
Per serving: 259 calories, 5 g protein, 48 g carbohydrates, 3 g fat (1 g saturated), 12 mg cholesterol, 114 mg sodium.

Pears in Beaujolais
Roland Passot

Here's a marvelous-tasting dessert that I remember from my boyhood in Lyons. It was made with a nice, light Beaujolais, the wine of the region. I still like to make it that way because Beaujolais goes so well with pears. The dish is easy, requiring little preparation. Serve it with a crisp *tuile*, or other cookie.

6 medium-size Bosc pears
3 cups Beaujolais wine
3/4 cup sugar
Zest of 1 orange
6 black peppercorns and 1 whole clove, tied in cheesecloth
1 cinnamon stick
1 vanilla bean
3/4 cup crème de cassis liqueur

Peel the pears carefully, leaving the stems intact. In a nonreactive saucepan, combine the wine, sugar and orange zest. Add the peppercorns and clove. Break the cinnamon stick in half and split the vanilla bean in two, and add them. Bring to a boil and let cook for 5 minutes over medium heat.

Place the pears in the wine, lower the heat and cook at a gentle simmer for 20 minutes, turning the pears frequently. Remove and discard the spices and let the pears cool in the wine syrup.

Stir the crème de cassis into the cooled syrup. Serve pears in dessert bowls with syrup spooned over them.

Yield: 6 servings.
Per serving: 394 calories, .8 g protein, 62 g carbohydrates, .6 g fat (0 g saturated), 0 mg cholesterol, 8 mg sodium.

Fruit Napoleon with Frozen Raspberry Yogurt
Kenneth Oringer

This is an alternative to a fresh fruit plate, and it's a lot more interesting. You can be as creative as you want with the architectural build-up of different fruits bound with frozen yogurt. And if you like, you can spoon a berry coulis over the dessert.

4 cups nonfat plain yogurt
1/2 cup honey
1 cup raspberries, puréed and strained
1 Red Delicious apple
1 Granny Smith apple
1 tablespoon fresh lemon juice
1 small honeydew melon, peeled, seeded and very
  thinly sliced
1 ripe mango, peeled and thinly sliced
1 cup strawberries, sliced
1 cup raspberries
1 cup blueberries
Fresh mint sprigs for garnish

In a large bowl, whisk together the yogurt, honey and raspberry purée, transfer to an ice cream maker and process according to the manufacturer's instructions. Store in a covered container in freezer until needed.

Cut the apples in half, core them, and slice the halves paper thin with a mandoline-style slicer or very sharp knife. Sprinkle lemon juice over the slices to prevent discoloring.

Assemble the napoleons on 4 dessert plates. Start with a circular layer of sliced apple, 3 inches in diameter, and alternate with layers of honeydew, mango and berries. Between each layer of fruit, place a 1/2-inch layer of frozen yogurt. Make 4 compact napoleons, about 3 inches high. Serve them chilled garnished with remaining berries and mint sprigs.

Yield: 4 servings.
Per serving: 397 calories, 14 g protein, 88 g carbohydrates, 1 g fat (.3 g saturated), 4 mg cholesterol, 183 mg sodium.

GUILT-FREE COOKIES
Barbara Karoff

A plate of cookies makes a fine and simple dessert. These fruit-studded, sugarless gems are a perfect dessert or between-meal snack.

½ cup dried apricots, cut up
½ cup golden raisins
½ cup dates, cut up
¾ cup (6-ounce can) orange juice concentrate
1 ½ cups rolled oats
1 cup whole wheat flour
½ teaspoon salt
1 teaspoon baking soda
1 egg, lightly beaten
½ cup canola oil or safflower oil
¼ cup sunflower seeds
¼ cup sesame seeds
Parchment paper

In a small nonreactive saucepan, combine the apricots, raisins, dates and orange juice concentrate. Simmer over low heat for 10 minutes. Cool.

Combine the oats, flour, salt and baking soda in a large bowl. Add the egg and oil and mix until well blended. Stir in the cooled fruit and the seeds.

Preheat the oven to 350 degrees F. Drop the batter by spoonfuls onto a parchment-lined baking sheet. Using a spatula, flatten to ¼-inch thickness. Bake in the oven for 12 to 15 minutes. Cool on a rack and store in an airtight container.

Yield: about 2 dozen cookies.
Per cookie: 126 calories, 3 g protein, 20 g carbohydrates, 6 g fat (.6 saturated), 8 mg cholesterol, 83 mg sodium.

PINK GRAPEFRUIT MERINGUE WITH RASPBERRIES AND HAZELNUTS
David Coyle

This dish is an adaptation of a French recipe made with oranges. I use pink grapefruit, which is sweeter than white, to produce a light, pleasing dessert. It's lovely-looking, great for parties and exceptionally refreshing.

3 large pink grapefruit
3 cups fresh raspberries
1 ⅓ cups superfine sugar
2 tablespoons Grand Marnier or kirsch liqueur
4 egg whites
¼ cup coarsely chopped hazelnuts

Cut 2 grapefruit in half with a serrated edge by making slanted cuts at 45-degree angles in a seesaw fashion with a sharp paring knife. Remove the seeds with the tip of the knife. Then, remove grapefruit segments, using a grapefruit or paring knife. Separate the segments from the membranes and place in a bowl. Cut the third grapefruit in half, but don't bother to serrate the edges, since you only need 4 decorative halves. Extract the segments in the same manner, and add to the bowl. Set aside the segments and the 4 serrated shells.

In a food processor or blender, purée 2 cups of the raspberries with ⅓ cup of the sugar and the Grand Marnier or kirsch. Press through a strainer to remove the seeds, working with a rubber spatula to get all the juice. Pour the raspberry purée over the grapefruit segments and gently mix together. Divide grapefruit segments among the 4 grapefruit shells. Top with remaining raspberries.

Preheat the oven to 450 degrees F. In the bowl of an electric mixer fitted with a whip attachment, beat the egg whites to soft peaks, and, with the machine still running, add 1 cup sugar a little at a time. Beat until the meringue is stiff and shiny.

Using a pastry bag, pipe the meringue in an attractive pattern around the top of the grapefruit halves. If you don't do the piping, spoon it on neatly. Sprinkle chopped hazelnuts over the meringue. Place grapefruit meringues on a baking sheet and bake in the oven until the meringue starts to brown, about 3 minutes. Serve on dessert plates.

Yield: 4 servings.
Per serving: 421 calories, 6 g protein, 88 g carbohydrates, 5 g fat (.3 g saturated), 0 mg cholesterol, 55 mg sodium.

MINTED CITRUS COMPOTE
Lindsey Shere

Here is a recipe I worked out for a delicious and slightly different kind of fruit compote to make in the winter. The combination of citrus, dates and mint satisfies the sweet tooth without any fat, although if you serve it with cookies, that will change the fat equation. The citrus I suggest are Lavender Gems (a grapefruit-tangerine hybrid), tangelos and blood oranges. But others may be used—for example, pink grapefruit, Valencia or navel oranges. As for the mint leaves, I use peppermint from my garden, but spearmint would be nicer, contributing a stronger flavor to the compote.

SYRUP
³/₄ cup water
¹/₄ cup sugar
10 to 12 fresh mint leaves

2 pounds assorted citrus fruit (such as Lavender Gems,
*   tangelos and blood oranges)*
2 to 3 kumquats
Another 10 to 12 fresh mint leaves
3 to 4 black dates (or a more familiar variety, like Medjool)
*   halved and pitted*

To prepare the syrup simmer the water, sugar and mint leaves over low heat in a covered saucepan for about 20 minutes. Discard the mint leaves and chill the syrup in the refrigerator.

Cut the skins from the citrus, taking care to remove the bitter white pith just under the skins. Slice the citrus ¹/₄ inch thick (except for Lavender Gems, if you are using them, and kumquats), and remove the seeds and white cores. Slices from large fruit should be halved or even quartered. Section the Lavender Gems (or pink grapefruit, if using) after peeling. Work over a bowl to catch the juice while sectioning and removing membrane. Slice the kumquats crosswise into very thin slices and seed them.

Stack the additional mint leaves and slice them into very thin shreds.

Layer the individual fruit in a serving bowl, alternating the different types of fruit and sprinkling each layer with shreds of mint. Pour the chilled syrup and accumulated juice over the fruit and garnish with the halved, pitted dates.

Yield: 4 servings.
Per serving: 268 calories, 1 g protein, 69 g carbohydrates, .3 g fat (.05 g saturated), 0 mg cholesterol, 2 mg sodium.

CRANBERRY SOUP WITH FRESH FRUIT
David Kinch

This was a very popular dessert when I was at Ernie's, served as a cold fruit soup or made into a sorbet. The cranberries may be fresh or frozen. Both work equally well, making this a delightful year-round dish.

1 pound fresh or frozen cranberries
1 cup honey
2 cups water
¾ cup white wine
Zest of ½ lemon
Zest of ½ lime
Zest of ½ orange
3 whole cloves
½ cinnamon stick
4 cups assorted ripe seasonal fruit (such as pineapple,
*   kiwifruit, grapes, raspberries, blueberries or other*
*   berries), cut into bite-size pieces*
Fresh mint leaves for garnish

Place the cranberries, honey and the water in a nonreactive saucepan. Bring to a boil, lower heat and cook at a gentle simmer until the liquid is reduced by half.

While cranberries are cooking, combine the wine, citrus zests, cloves and cinnamon in another nonreactive saucepan and cook over medium heat until reduced by half.

Strain the cranberry liquid through a colander into a bowl and let drain completely without pressing the berries. This will prevent the broth from becoming cloudy. Discard the cranberries or use for another purpose.

Strain the spiced wine mixture through a fine sieve directly into the cranberry broth and stir until the two liquids are well blended. Let cool.

Ladle the cranberry soup into soup bowls. Top with seasonal fruit. Garnish with mint leaves.

Yield: six 1-cup servings.
Per serving: 284 calories, .1 g protein, 70 g carbohydrates, .7 g fat (.1 g saturated), 0 mg cholesterol, 7 mg sodium.

CHOLESTEROL-FREE RASPBERRY SOUFFLÉ
Gary Danko

I came up with this recipe in Vermont when I was working at a country inn called Tucker Hill. We made our own jam and had a lot of it, so I started making mousses. Then, one day, I decided to try baking the mousse as a soufflé made only with egg whites folded into a viscous base. It could not be simpler to make, and people can use any jam they have in the cupboard, not just raspberry. Besides, it's completely free of cholesterol.

Vegetable oil spray and sugar to coat soufflé dishes
1 cup sieved raspberry jam (measure after sieving)
1 tablespoon Grand Marnier, kirsch or liqueur of choice
6 egg whites

RASPBERRY SAUCE
1 pint fresh raspberries
1 tablespoon sugar
1 tablespoon Grand Marnier or kirsch

Prepare six 6-ounce (³/₄ cup) soufflé dishes by spraying with vegetable oil spray and coating with sugar. Set aside.

In a large bowl, whisk together the jam and liqueur until smooth. In the bowl of an electric mixer or with a whisk, beat the egg whites to mounding peaks. Fold the beaten egg whites into the jam mixture until just combined. Fill soufflé dishes and level off the top. This may be done up to 1 hour before baking. If so, cover the uncooked soufflés with plastic wrap and refrigerate.

To prepare the raspberry sauce, heat the raspberries, sugar and liqueur in a small saucepan over medium heat until the sugar dissolves and the mixture is bubbling, about 5 minutes. Remove from the heat and cool. Serve it chunky or purée in a blender or food processor and sieve out the seeds. Set aside.

Preheat the oven to 350 degrees F. Place the soufflés on a baking sheet and bake on the middle shelf of the oven until the tops have risen and are golden brown, 10 to 15 minutes. Remove and serve immediately with raspberry sauce.

Yield: 6 servings.
Per serving: 214 calories, 4 g protein, 48 g carbohydrates, .2 g fat (0 g saturated), 0 mg cholesterol, 61 mg sodium.

GAZPACHO FRUIT SOUP
Roland Passot

This variation on a chilled gazpacho soup consists of a rich wine and berry syrup and an assortment of diced fresh fruit and berries. Choose your own mix of fruit, depending on availability. Summer is the best time for this soup, when berries are at their peak. Eat it outdoors when the weather is hot, and serve it ice cold.

2 bottles (750 ml each) red wine (preferably Pinot Noir)
³/₄ cup sugar
2 cinnamon sticks, 3 whole cloves, 30 black peppercorns and 2 ounces sliced fresh ginger, tied in cheesecloth.
¹/₂ cup puréed fresh or frozen raspberries
¹/₂ cup puréed fresh or frozen blackberries
¹/₂ cup puréed red currants (if available)
¹/₂ cup crème de cassis liqueur

SUGGESTED DICED FRUIT AND BERRIES
FOR TOTAL OF 8 CUPS
¹/₂ cantaloupe, peeled, seeded and diced
1 ripe mango, peeled and diced
1 kiwifruit, peeled and diced
1 pineapple, peeled, cored and diced
1 cup blueberries
1 cup blackberries
1 cup raspberries
1 cup fresh quartered figs (if available)

Nonfat plain yogurt or frozen yogurt and fresh mint sprigs for garnish

In a large heavy-bottomed, nonreactive saucepan, bring the wine and sugar to a boil, lower heat and cook the mixture over medium heat until it is reduced by half and syrupy. Remove from heat, add the cheesecloth packet of spices and let them infuse in the wine syrup for 10 minutes. Then remove and discard spices.

Add the puréed berries and crème de cassis to the syrup, bring to a boil over medium heat, lower heat and simmer for 5 minutes. Strain the mixture into a bowl. Cover and place in refrigerator to chill.

Serve the soup in bowls with fresh diced fruit, garnished with a dollop of frozen yogurt and a mint sprig.

Yield: eight 1 ¹/₃-cup servings.
Per serving: 414 calories, 3 g protein, 60 g carbohydrates, 1 g fat (.1 g saturated), .5 mg cholesterol, 43 mg sodium.

RICOTTA AL CAFFÈ
Carlo Middione

This light, refreshing dessert will give you the impression you're eating something much more sinful than it is. The proportions for the recipe are approximate. You may use amounts that please you. The only critical thing is to be sure the ricotta mixture remains firm enough to spoon into serving glasses. It should not be runny by any means.

1 pound low-fat ricotta cheese
1 tablespoon cocoa powder
Zest of 1/2 lemon, grated or minced
1/4 cup cold espresso coffee
1/2 cup chestnut honey (or honey of your preference)
Fresh berries or sliced fruit (such as pears or apples that
*   are not too tart) for garnish*
Cookies or anise-flavored biscotti (optional)
*   for accompaniment*

   In a large bowl, gently mix the ricotta, cocoa, lemon zest and espresso coffee in folding motions. Cover and refrigerate for a few hours for best results.
   Spoon the mixture into small glasses or *pot de crème* cups. Pass the honey to be drizzled over the top. Garnish with fresh berries or sliced fruit. If you want a more substantial dessert, you should pass some plain cookies or anise-flavored biscotti.

Yield: 6 servings.
Per serving: 190 calories, .2 g protein, 23 g carbohydrates, 5 g fat (2 g saturated), 25 mg cholesterol, 58 mg sodium.

CHARDONNAY SORBET
Gérald Hirigoyen

Since so many people relate to Chardonnay, I thought it would be fun to put it into a sorbet. I wanted something light and not too sweet that could cleanse the palate after a heavy meal. Serve it with fresh berries or other fruit. But please note that this sorbet is very fragile due to the alcoholic content. It is best to serve it right away, since even in the freezer, the creamy texture will not hold up for longer than one day. After that, the sorbet tends to separate.

1 1/2 cups sugar
1 1/2 cups water
1/2 split vanilla bean
1/2 lime
1/4 lemon
1/4 orange
1 bottle (750 ml) Chardonnay

   Place the sugar, water and vanilla bean in a saucepan. Drop in the pieces of lime, lemon and orange. Bring the mixture to a boil, reduce heat, and let simmer for 5 minutes, taking care only to infuse flavor and not to reduce the liquid.
   Strain the mixture into a bowl. Add the Chardonnay, mix and cover. Let the mixture cool in the refrigerator for at least 2 hours. Transfer the cooled mixture to an ice cream maker and process according to the manufacturer's instructions. Process until the sorbet is smooth and creamy. Serve immediately or store in the freezer for no more than a day.

Yield: about 3 pints or six 1 1/s-cup servings.
Per serving: 455 calories, .4 g protein, 78 g carbohydrates, 0 g fat (0 g saturated), 0 mg cholesterol, 13 mg sodium.

9
basics

STOCKS

Beef or Veal Stock and Demi-Glace
Chicken Stock
Fish Stock
Vegetable Stock

TECHNIQUES AND TERMINOLOGY

✳

BEEF OR VEAL STOCK AND DEMI-GLACE

In classic French cooking, beef or veal stock is made by a lengthy process, and when it is reduced by half, the richer stock is called demi-glace (half-glaze) which is used for innumerable sauces. Since stock and demi-glace are skimmed of all fat when they are prepared, they are virtually fat free. A frozen, unsalted demi-glace with less than 1 gram of fat is available in 8-ounce containers labeled "rich beef stock" at better markets.

6 pounds beef or veal shanks and marrow bones,
* cracked and cut up by the butcher*
About 8 quarts cold water
2 medium-size yellow onions, coarsely chopped
1 leek (white part only), well washed and coarsely
* chopped (optional)*
2 large carrots, coarsely chopped
2 stalks celery, coarsely chopped
2 ripe tomatoes, cut up
3 cloves garlic, mashed
1 cup white wine
5 fresh parsley sprigs
8 black peppercorns
4 fresh thyme sprigs
2 bay leaves
1 small sprig fresh rosemary (optional)
2 whole cloves

Preheat the oven to 450 degrees F. Place the shanks and bones in a large roasting pan and roast, turning occasionally with metal tongs, until browned but not scorched.

Transfer the bones to a stockpot, cover with the cold water, bring to a boil, reduce heat and simmer uncovered for 1 to 2 hours. Skim scum from surface with skimmer or large metal spoon.

Meanwhile, place the roasting pan with fat on top of the stove and brown the vegetables over moderate heat, about 10 minutes. Vegetables should be caramelized but not scorched. Transfer vegetables to the stockpot. Pour out fat from the pan and discard. Pour the white wine into the pan and bring to a boil, scraping up the browned bits on the bottom of the pan. Add these pan juices and remaining ingredients to the stockpot.

Simmer the stock uncovered over very low heat for at least 6 hours or all day.

With a slotted spoon or skimmer, remove solids from the stock. Pour the stock through a strainer into a large non-reactive container. Allow to cool, then cover and refrigerate. When cold, remove the layer of fat from the top with a spoon and discard. Store in refrigerator or freeze in small batches to use as needed.

For demi-glace, boil the stock uncovered over medium or low heat until reduced by half. Let cool, cover and refrigerate. Freeze, if you wish, in small batches.

Yield: about 5 quarts stock or 1 ½ quarts demi-glace.

CHICKEN STOCK

Chicken stock is easy to make and may be frozen in small amounts to use as needed. When well skimmed, it should be virtually fat free. A frozen, unsalted rich chicken stock with less than 1 gram of fat is available in 8-ounce containers at better markets.

5 pounds chicken parts (carcasses, backs, wings, necks, feet)
About 5 quarts cold water
1 large yellow onion, coarsely chopped
1 medium-size carrot, sliced
2 stalks celery, coarsely chopped
2 bay leaves
2 sprigs fresh thyme
4 sprigs fresh parsley
1 clove garlic, mashed
1 sprig fresh rosemary (optional)
6 white peppercorns (if necessary, black peppercorns
* may be substituted)*
2 whole cloves

basics

147

Place the chicken parts in a stockpot and cover with the water. Bring to a boil over high heat. As soon as it boils, lower heat and skim off the scum from the surface. Add all the remaining ingredients and simmer, uncovered, over very low heat for 3 hours. Strain the stock, discarding the solids, and let cool. Refrigerate until cold, then remove the layer of fat from the top with a spoon and discard. The stock will keep 4 or 5 days, covered, in the refrigerator. Freeze, if you wish, in small batches to use as needed. For a rich stock, gently boil the stock over low to medium heat until reduced by half.

Yield: about 4 quarts stock or 2 quarts rich stock.

FISH STOCK

For a good fish stock, use bones from nonoily whitefish (e.g., sole, halibut, grouper, bass). The stock should be simmered no more than 40 minutes, and the vegetables cut small so they cook through in the short cooking time. A frozen, unsalted fish stock is sold in better markets in 8-ounce containers. In a pinch, bottled clam juice diluted with water may be substituted for fish stock.

5 pounds bones, heads and skins from nonoily whitefish
1 cup chopped yellow onion
1 cup chopped celery
2 bay leaves
1 sprig fresh thyme
2 sprigs fresh parsley
1 sprig fresh tarragon
4 whole white peppercorns (if necessary, black peppercorns may be substituted)
4 quarts cold water
1 cup white wine

Wash the fish bones, remove gills from the heads and scrape away under water any blood from the carcasses. Place the onion, celery and herbs in a stockpot with 1 cup of water, cover, and sweat the mixture over low heat for 10 minutes. Add the fish bones and remaining water. Bring to a boil, lower the heat and skim off any scum from surface. Simmer uncovered over very low heat for 20 minutes. Add the wine and simmer another 20 minutes. Strain, discarding the solids. Allow to cool, then cover and refrigerate. Freeze, if you wish, in small batches.

Yield: about 3 quarts.

VEGETABLE STOCK

This is a good, basic, full-flavored vegetable stock that will keep for up to four days in the refrigerator, or longer, if frozen. If you're in a hurry, Swanson's vegetable broth is sold in 14 1/2-ounce cans at most supermarkets.

1 medium-size yellow onion, quartered
3 carrots, sliced
4 medium-size ripe tomatoes, halved
1 fennel bulb, coarsely chopped
1 leek (white part only), washed and sliced
1/2 bay leaf
2 sprigs fresh thyme
1 teaspoon chopped fresh marjoram
6 fresh parsley stems
Salt and freshly ground pepper to taste
8 cups cold water

Combine all the ingredients in a large saucepan or stockpot. Bring to a boil, reduce heat and gently simmer over low heat for 45 minutes. Strain the stock through a fine strainer. Cool to room temperature, then cover and store in the refrigerator or freeze in small batches for use as needed.

Yield: about 6 cups.

BASIL OIL

In a medium-size saucepan, blanch 1 bunch fresh basil (including stems) in boiling water for 15 seconds. Remove to a colander and refresh under cold running water. Drain well and pat dry with a towel. Measure the blanched basil in a measuring cup, then place in a blender or food processor and add an equal amount of olive oil. Blend to a smooth paste. Transfer to a jar and add 3 times as much olive oil as basil paste. Mix thoroughly, cover and store for a day. When the basil has separated from the oil, filter the oil through a paper coffee filter or 2 layers of cheesecloth. Use as needed or store, covered, in refrigerator for up to 1 week.

CURRY OIL

In a glass or clear plastic jar, mix 3 tablespoons curry powder with 1 tablespoon water to a smooth paste and add 2 cups canola oil. Cover tightly and shake to mix. Set aside for 2 days, shaking the jar occasionally to remix oil. With a ladle or spoon, remove oil from jar, being careful not to remove curry solids that have settled at the bottom of jar. Discard the solids. Strain the oil through a paper coffee filter or 2 layers of cheesecloth. The curry oil may be stored, tightly covered, in the refrigerator for up to 6 months.

GARLIC, ROASTED

Roasted garlic has a mild, sweet flavor that is especially pleasing for lightly cooked dishes or to spread on French bread. To roast garlic, place unpeeled cloves in a small baking pan. Brush them lightly with olive oil or use olive-oil spray. Place in a preheated 350-degree F. oven until the garlic is soft, about 30 minutes. Once the garlic has cooled, remove the skin and, if you wish, mash the pulp with a fork into a paste. You may also roast the whole garlic bulb and store the leftover paste in the refrigerator. Cut the bulb in half horizontally, brush each half with olive oil and season it, if you wish, with salt and pepper and fresh or dried thyme. Roast for 30 minutes until soft. Squeeze each half to remove the pulp.

GINGER JUICE

Ginger juice is used for Asian-style marinades and sauces. To prepare it, grate or finely chop fresh ginger (a food processor works best), wrap it in a clean kitchen towel or cheesecloth and squeeze out the juice. For 1 tablespoon juice, use 1 1/2 ounces ginger.

GLASS OR CELLOPHANE NOODLES

Glass or cellophane noodles are very thin Asian noodles that turn translucent and glisten like glass after cooking. The Chinese make them with mung bean flour and call them mung bean threads. The Japanese call theirs *saifun* and make the noodles with sweet potato and white potato starch. Both kinds are opaque and white when dry. To soften them, they need to be cooked for 3 or 4 minutes in boiling water for use in soups, salads and stews. When soft and translucent, they absorb the flavors of any rich broth or sauce. Available in Asian markets, they come in different size cellophane bags. An 8-ounce package is sufficient for 4 to 6 servings.

Kaffir Lime Leaves

Kaffir lime is indigenous to Southeast Asia. The fruit (dark green with a wartlike rind) has very fragrant leaves which are popular as a seasoning in Thai cooking. The leaves are mostly available dried, but may occasionally be found fresh or frozen in Asian food stores. The dried leaves should be soaked about 5 minutes in warm water and may be used whole, like bay leaves, or finely chopped for soups, stews and other dishes.

Nuts and Seeds, Toasted

To toast macadamia nuts, pine nuts or pumpkin seeds, place them in an oven proof skillet and toast in a preheated 350-degree F oven until they are golden brown, about 5 minutes. To toast sesame seeds, follow the same procedure, but toast 1 to 2 minutes. To toast anise, coriander or cumin seeds, place them in a dry skillet and toast on top of the stove over high heat until they are fragrant and begin to smoke and pop, 1 to 2 minutes. To crush or grind the seeds, use a mortar and pestle or spice grinder.

Red Bell Peppers, Roasted

Some chefs like to roast red bell peppers slowly by placing them on a baking sheet in a preheated 375-degree F. oven until the peppers blister and start to blacken, about 30 minutes. Others prefer a faster method and char the peppers under a broiler or over a direct flame on top of the stove, turning them often with tongs until they are blackened on all sides. After the peppers are roasted, transfer them to a paper or plastic bag or to a plastic container with a lid. Close the bag tightly or cover the container and let the peppers steam for 20 minutes. Peel off the skins with your fingers. Scrape off any stubborn black pieces with a small knife. Cut the peppers in half, remove the stems, seeds and veins. Then, cut the peppers into strips, 1/4 to 1/2 inch wide, and use as needed.

Sichuan Peppercorns

One of the oldest Chinese spices, Sichuan peppercorns are not related to black peppercorns and their use is not limited to Sichuan cuisine. Brown or reddish in color, they are aromatic and very pungent and actually numb the tongue. You'll find them in the spice section of Chinese food stores in plastic bags, often with no English markings and more often with small twigs and leaves mixed in with the peppercorns. Before using, sort them, then toast them to smoking in a dry skillet over high heat for 2 minutes. To grind, use a spice grinder or mortar and pestle.

Sushi Rice

Sushi rice is a stubby rice often labeled "medium grain." It's available in Japanese and other Asian food stores, and some supermarkets. To cook, combine 1 cup rice and 1 1/2 cups water in a medium-size saucepan. Bring to a boil, reduce heat; cover tightly and simmer until the rice is tender, about 20 minutes. Do not uncover during cooking. When done, let stand covered for 10 minutes. Fluff with a fork. Makes 3 cups of cooked sushi rice. This amount is usually seasoned with 2 tablespoons rice vinegar, 3/4 teaspoon salt, 1 tablespoon granulated sugar and 1 teaspoon wasabi (Japanese horseradish). For sushi, it's rolled inside sheets of nori (dried seaweed) or shaped with the hands into small rectangles (2 tablespoons each) that are topped with different fish.

153

Table of Equivalents

The exact equivalents in the following tables have been rounded for convenience.

US/UK

oz=ounce
lb=pound
in=inch
ft=foot
tbl=tablespoon
fl oz=fluid ounce
qt=quart

Metric

g=gram
kg=kilogram
mm=millimeter
cm=centimeter
ml=milliliter
l=liter

Weights

US/UK	Metric
1 oz	30 g
2 oz	60 g
3 oz	90 g
4 oz ($^1/_4$ lb)	125 g
5 oz ($^1/_3$ lb)	155 g
6 oz	185 g
7 oz	220 g
8 oz ($^1/_2$ lb)	250 g
10 oz	315 g
12 oz ($^3/_4$ lb)	375 g
14 oz	440 g
16 oz (1 lb)	500 g
$1^1/_2$ lb	750 g
2 lb	1 kg
3 lb	1.5 kg

Oven Temperatures

Fahrenheit	Celsius	Gas
250	120	$^1/_2$
275	140	1
300	150	2
325	160	3
350	180	4
375	190	5
400	200	6
425	220	7
450	230	8
475	240	9
500	260	10

Liquids

US	Metric	UK
2 tbl	30 ml	1 fl oz
$^1/_4$ cup	60 ml	2 fl oz
$^1/_3$ cup	80 ml	3 fl oz
$^1/_2$ cup	125 ml	4 fl oz
$^2/_3$ cup	160 ml	5 fl oz
$^3/_4$ cup	180 ml	6 fl oz
1 cup	250 ml	8 fl oz
$1^1/_2$ cups	375 ml	12 fl oz
2 cups	500 ml	16 fl oz
4 cups/1 qt	1 l	32 fl oz

Length Measures

$^1/_8$ in	3 mm
$^1/_4$ in	6 mm
$^1/_2$ in	12 mm
1 in	2.5 cm
2 in	5 cm
3 in	7.5 cm
4 in	10 cm
5 in	13 cm
6 in	15 cm
7 in	18 cm
8 in	20 cm
9 in	23 cm
10 in	25 cm
11 in	28 cm
12/1 ft	30 cm